THE FRONTIERS OF
FARCE

Other Plays by Peter Barnes

The Ruling Class

Noonday Demons and
Leonardo's Last Supper

Lulu

The Bewitched

The Frontiers of Farce

ADAPTATIONS
by
PETER BARNES
of

George Feydeau's
The Purging

Frank Wedekind's
The Singer

HEINEMANN
LONDON

Heinemann Educational Books Ltd
LONDON   EDINBURGH   MELBOURNE   TORONTO
JOHANNESBURG   NEW DELHI   AUCKLAND
SINGAPORE   HONG KONG   NAIROBI
IBADAN   KUALA LUMPUR   KINGSTON

ISBN
0 435 23063 8

Published by
Heinemann Educational Books Ltd
48 Charles Street, London W1X 8AH
Set in 10/11pt Garamond by
Spectrum Typesetting, London
and printed in Great Britain by
Biddles of Guildford

CONTENTS

To Dilys

INTRODUCTION

The last complete plays Georges Feydeau wrote alone were four
ferocious one-act pieces which included *The Purging* (*On purge
Bébé* 1910). In 1909 Feydeau had quarrelled violently with his
wife Marianne and left her. They were divorced a few years later.
The untamed shrew in *The Purging* is reputedly based on
Marianne. Subsequently Feydeau was discovered to be suffering
from venereal disease. His sons put him in an asylum where he
ended up thinking he was Napoleon III and sending out
invitations to his coronation. He died on 5 June 1921.

The later Feydeau plays strip away the false romanticism of
'Oo la-la and Gay Paree' which he himself, to some extent,
helped to create, and show us instead that a Frenchman's main
concern is not sex but money and the state of his bowels.

This is the play Strindberg did not write, a scene Bergman left
out of *Scenes from a Marriage*, a farcical illustration of the bleak
dictum that husbands and wives are separated by nothing but
marriage.

Feydeau's anti-romantic vision is matched by Frank
Wedekind's in *The Singer* (*Der Kammersänger* 1897). With his
abrupt changes of mood and style Wedekind is one of the
fathers of modern theatre. He helped revolutionize sexual
morality, and his attack on the sentimental humbug
surrounding art is equally ruthless.

His mother was a Hungarian opera-singer and in the flood
tide of Wagner-fever, when all roads led to Bayreuth and
Valhalla, Wedekind pointed out the reality behind the
pretensions of high culture: that even here everything is still
'addition and subtraction, the rest is conversation'. The adored

tenor (a pop star with class) battered by rapacious art-lovers and would-be artists, tries with increasing desperation to make them see he is as much a wage slave as any factory worker. Once again, even in the glamorous world of the opera, the capital ethos still prevails, seeking to substitute monetary values for human and artistic ones.

The first full professional production of these plays in this country took place at the Old Vic in October 1976. They are both on the outer limits of farce where everything is pushed to extremes of pain and cruelty, which is the very source of both the comic and the tragic.

P.B.

THE PURGING

by
Georges Feydeau

CHARACTERS

FOLLAVOINE
ROSE
JULIE
CHOUILLOUX
BABY
MADAME CHOUILLOUX
TRUCHET

Paris 1904

The Purging was first presented by James Verner at the Old Vic Theatre, London, on 11 October 1976, with the following cast:

Follavoine	Leonard Rossiter
Rose	Joan Morrow
Julie	Dilys Laye
Chouilloux	John Phillips
Baby	Adam Armstrong
Madame Chouilloux	Penny Ryder
Truchet	William Sleigh

Directed by **Peter Barnes**
Designed by Michael Annals
Lighting by Leonard Tucker

THE PURGING

Follavoine's *study. Double doors to the hall Up Stage Centre. On each side of them a large cabinet with opaque fronts, made of glass. Window Stage Left and a large, cluttered desk. Down Stage Right a side door to the bedroom. Above it Stage Right a sofa.*

Follavoine *is seated at the desk, looking through a large dictionary.*

Follavoine: Azores . . . the Azores *(there is a knock on the door)* Come in.

    Rose, *the maid, enters Up Stage Centre.*

Rose: Madam wishes to see you Monsieur.

Follavoine: She knows where I am . . . the Azores.

Rose: Madam's in the bathroom. She's too busy to come.

Follavoine: So am I. Tell her I'm working . . . Rose, don't forget to show Monsieur Chouilloux in the moment he arrives. Wait a minute. While you're here . . . the Azores? The Azores? Do you happen to know where they are?

Rose: Not me Monsieur! Madam doesn't let me put things away. You can't blame . . .

Follavoine: Put things away? What you babbling about? The Azores! They're islands. *Islands*—earth surrounded by water. You know what earth surrounded by water is?

Rose: Mud?

Follavoine: MUD?! So much for the French education system. *Mud* is a little earth and a little water. Islands're a lot of earth and a lot of water. All salt. The Azores. You understand? They're not in the house.

3

Rose: Oh they're outside?

Follavoine: Of course they're outside.

Rose: Then I haven't seen them. I haven't been in Paris long. I'm from . . .

Follavoine (*guiding her to the door Down Stage Right*): I know. I know.

Rose: I can't get out much with only one half day off a week. I couldn't see the Azores in a half-day. It's not even a half-day. By the time I've finished serving luncheon it's gone three and . . .

Follavoine: Absolutely . . . (*he pushes her out*) Stupid girl. Illiterate to her knee-caps. *Mud.* (*he goes back to the dictionary*) Now . . . Azores . . . (*reading*) 'O-Z-O . . . Ozomose: root-rot caused by parasitic fungus which attacks both plants and trees such as the apple, cotton, elm, lime and pear . . .' but not the Azores. Where are they? (*reading*) 'Ozostomia: offensive breath due to foulness of the mouth or to disease. Greek ozo meaning smell plus stoma meaning, mouth.' Useless. USELESS. (*he snaps the dictionary shut*) That's what comes of buying a cheap dictionary. No sense of the priorities. They include a word like Ozostomia and leave out the Azores.

> **Follavoine**'s *wife,* **Julie,** *hurries in Down Stage Right, dressed in a dirty bathrobe. Her hair is in curlers, her stockings are down round her ankles and she carries a bucket of dirty water.*

Julie: So you're too busy to speak to me?

Follavoine: Too busy to come running every time you call.

Julie: If I were somebody else's wife you'd come running.

Follavoine: If you were somebody else's wife . . . Ah yes . . . well you're not and there's an end of it. I'm busy I tell you.

Julie (*putting her bucket on the floor*): Busy? How can you be busy? You've got nothing to be busy about.

Follavoine (*pointing at the bucket*): What's that doing here?!

Julie: I'm going to empty it.

Follavoine: In my study?

Julie: No, fathead. I had it in my hand when Rose came back with your charming reply. I knew I couldn't keep his lordship waiting when he was so busy. What you so busy with?

Follavoine: Things.

Julie: Things? What things?

Follavoine: Things.

Julie: *Things.* Yes things are just the sort of things that would keep you busy.

Follavoine: Yes things. I was looking up the Azores in the dictionary if you must know. Satisfied?

Julie: The Azores? You're going there I suppose?

Follavoine: I've thought of it, often.

Julie: Premature senility. What's a porcelain manufacturer want to look up the Azores for?

Follavoine: I don't give a damn about the Azores. It's for Baby. Children think their fathers know everything.

Julie: He must've found out by now it's not true in your case.

Follavoine (*imitating his son*): 'Dadda, Dadda, where's the Azores . . . ?' (*his own voice*) 'The what, son . . . ?' (*son's voice*) 'The Azores, Dadda, the Azores.' Actually I heard him the first time. How should I know where some unknown islands are? They're not even French.

Julie: You shouldn't show your ignorance in front of Baby.

Follavoine: *You* know where they are I suppose?

Julie: Yes I think . . . I've seen them . . . on a map . . . I don't exactly remember . . .

Follavoine: You don't know, blockhead. You don't exactly remember? *Ha!* And again, *ha!*

Julie: What did you tell Baby?

Follavoine: I used my imagination. I said 'You mustn't ask questions like that. The Azores aren't for children'.

Julie: Brilliant! 'The Azores aren't for children.' You quarter-wit!

Follavoine: A quarter-wit am I? Do you know what an ozonise is? Root-rot caused by parasitic fungus which attacks plant and trees. Ha! And ozostomia? What about ozostomia? That's offensive breath. Ozonise and ozostomia, words everyone knows. Except you, stupid.

Julie: What about the Azores?

Follavoine: It was one of the questions in Baby's geography lesson. Cluttering up the boy's mind with worthless junk.

With railways and boats to take you anywhere you want to go. Who needs geography nowadays? You just look up a timetable.

Julie: So that's how you help your son. 'Where's the Azores, Dadda?' 'Go look up a timetable.'

Follavoine: I didn't say that. I made out as if I really knew the answer but didn't want to say. 'It's better if you try and find out for yourself. If you really can't then I'll tell you.' Then I closed the door and grabbed the dictionary.

Julie: Well where are the Azores?

Follavoine: Nowhere. It's not in there.

Julie: Nowhere? Let me look.

She opens the dictionary at the page with the bookmark.

Follavoine: You won't find it. I've rechecked a dozen times.

Julie *(reading)*: Ozonise . . . Ozost . . . *(she begins laughing sarcastically)*

Follavoine: What's so funny?

Julie: You. You've been looking under O.

Follavoine: Yes O for Azores.

Julie: No wonder you couldn't find it. You cretin.

Follavoine: Not O? If it isn't O, where is it?

Julie *(turning to another page)*: You'll see. O for Azores . . . An illiterate. A fully functioning illiterate. Thank God Baby's . . . Illegitimate'.

Follavoine: What?!

Julie: How can they have such words in a respectable dictionary? Somebody should complain. *(she reads)* 'Iznik: a village in Turkey. Izolta: same as Iseult an Irish princess beloved by Tristan. Izote . . .' Hhhm . . . Odd . . .

Follavoine: What? What?

Julie: It's not here.

Follavoine: *Ah!* Didn't I tell you? But you knew better. Oh yes, you know it all!

Julie: It should be between 'Izolta' and 'Izote'.

Follavoine: That dictionary is useless. USELESS. You can look for the Azores under any letter you please, it's not there. I kept telling you but you never listen.

Julie: Well at least I looked under I. That's a lot more logical than O.

Follavoine: A lot more logical than O! Why should I be more logical than O, U or even A? A's *very* logical for Azores don't you think?!

Julie: What do you mean A's for Azores . . .? A . . . wait a minute . . . Azores *(she turns the pages)* A . . . A . . . A . . .

Follavoine: A-A-A-A-A-A-A-A.

Julie *(reading)*: 'Azonic . . . Azoology . . .' Ahh I've found it! Azores.

Follavoine: You've found it?!

Julie: See! 'Island in the North Atlantic. A province of Portugal.'

Follavoine *(looking over her shoulder)*: Absolutely!

Julie: '922 square miles in area. Capital Ponta Delgada.'

Follavoine: Ponta Delgada. I didn't know that. You learn something new every minute of the day.

Julie: We'd never've found it under the O's or I's. *(she picks up her bucket)* It was right there under the A's all the time.

Follavoine: Just like I said.

Julie: Like you said?

Follavoine: Didn't I say it?

Julie: Yes, but you didn't mean it.

Follavoine: Didn't mean it? I always mean what I say.

Julie: You were making fun of me. You said A's more logical for Azores, don't you think?

Follavoine: A was more logical for Azores, as you've just proved.

Julie: *I* found it . . .!

Follavoine: Who told you where to look?

Julie *(shaking the bucket in fury)*: I found it! I found it!

Follavoine *(taking the bucket from her)*: All right you found it. You found it. *(He looks around with the bucket)*

Julie: What you doing?

Follavoine: Nothing. Looking for a place to put this down.

Julie: On the floor, numskull. *(he puts the bucket down on the floor)* You've got a nerve, claiming you found the Azores. *I* found it!

Follavoine: Right. You found it. Just you, you, you. You alone, Madame. Nobody else but you. Now for God's sake go and get dressed. It's gone eleven. Monsieur Chouilloux and his

wife will be here any minute and you're still running around
in that filthy bathrobe . . .

Julie: That's right, change the subject.

Follavoine: Curlers in what's left of your hair and stockings
round your ankles. Charming!

Julie (*pulling up her stockings*): There. Happy?

Follavoine: They won't stay up. Wear a corset, dammit.

Julie: When I'm cleaning the bath? Oh that's *clever*!
She picks up the bucket and moves to the door.

Follavoine: Why do *you* have to clean the bath?

Julie: Because it gets filthy and nobody else'll do it. (*she comes
back and puts down the bucket*) I have to do everything.
There is only me.

Follavoine: What about the maid?

Julie: The maid. Oh, yes, the maid.

Follavoine: Why've we got her if you still do the work?

Julie: She helps.

Follavoine: How?

Julie: Well, she watches me.

Follavoine: So I pay that moronic girl a huge salary to stand
around watching you work.

Julie: You don't pay me anything. So what difference does it
make if I do the housework instead of the maid?

Follavoine: It's obvious we don't need her.

Julie: You'd rather see me collapse than spend a few francs on a
maid! You skin-flint!

Follavoine: Pull up your stockings.

Julie (*she pulls her stockings and crosses to the desk*): All this
shouting . . .

Follavoine: I'm not shouting.

Julie: Just because I clean the bathroom myself. (*she starts
compulsively arranging the papers on his desk*) I thought
you'd be grateful. I suppose you'd like me to be like other
women out all day at the hairdresser's . . .

Follavoine: What you doing now?

Julie: At the dressmaker's . . .

Follavoine (*defending his papers*): Keep your hands off.

Julie: At the races . . .

Follavoine: Back, Madame. Back!

Julie: Out all day and night spending money.

Follavoine: Stop!

Julie: Expensive life you'd like me to lead I must say!

Follavoine: For God's sake woman! *(He pulls her away from his desk and papers)*

Julie: What is it?

Follavoine: My papers! Who asked you to touch them?

Julie: They were in a mess.

Follavoine: They are now. They're my papers, not yours. Mine, Madame!

Julie: Yours? Keep your assinine papers.

She starts to leave, taking her bucket as she goes.

Follavoine: Go mess up your own papers. Pick . . . pick . . . pick . . .

As he sits at his desk to sort out the papers, **Julie** *returns.*

Julie: That's how you'd like me to be isn't it?!

Follavoine: How I'd like you to be is invisible. What're you drivelling on about?

Julie: Like those other women.

Follavoine: What other women? I don't care! Only leave my papers alone in future. Don't touch them!

Julie *parades up and down, the bucket still dangling from her arm.*

Julie: Is this what you want? A lady. Oh yes, most definitely a lady. I could if I wanted, easy. But I haven't the time. I was expected to be useful. My family . . .

Follavoine: Yes I know.

Julie *places her bucket on some papers* **Follavoine** *is just about to sort out.*

Julie: My family didn't bring me up . . .

Follavoine: Madame; the bucket!

Julie *(picking up the bucket)*: To be a parasite. They taught me to be a good housewife.

Follavoine: Very interesting. But it's gone eleven and . . .

Julie: That's how I was brought up. In the best French bourgeois tradition. Not to depend on anyone to do my work for me. Because in life you can never tell when you may have to take care of yourself. We must all learn to be self-sufficient and clean out our own bathwater. Something you should think

9

about.

Follavoine: Your stockings!

Julie (*she pulls them up again*)**:** That's how my family brought me up. Now it's second nature. Right or wrong that's how I am. Independent. I take after my mother.

Follavoine: Ah yes . . . Mother-in-law . . .

Julie: No. My mother.

Follavoine: That's what I said.

Julie: No you didn't. When I say, my mother, it sounds tender and affectionate. When you say mother-in-law, it sounds mean and sarcastic.

Follavoine: Mother-in-law . . . Mother-in-law . . . Is that better? I mean she is my mother-in-law. If I say mother-in-law it's because she is. I'm stuck with her. As far as I'm concerned your mother is just . . .

Julie: My mother is what?!

Follavoine: I was going to say, your mother is just my . . .

Julie: Leave my mother alone. She's a marvellous woman and you're picking on her again. It's because I brought my bucket into your precious study isn't it?

Follavoine: No!

Julie: All this over a little bucket. See. I'm taking it away. Now you won't have anything to shout about.

Follavoine: Good.

> **Julie** *moves towards the door, stops, crosses back to the desk and puts the bucket in the same place as before.* **Follavoine** *groans.*

Julie: I'm not a criminal. Next time you want to find fault with me don't . . .

Follavoine: That damn bucket!

Julie: . . . drag my poor mother into it!

Follavoine: You're driving me mad! What did I say? What did I say?

Julie: What did I say? You know very well what you said!

Follavoine: I don't . . . Stop playing with my papers! And get out!

Julie: I like to see things in their proper place.

Follavoine: You like to see! What about *that*!

> *He hits the bucket on his desk.* **Julie** *picks it up.*

Julie: So . . .?

Follavoine: You like to see things in their proper place! If you're so neat, go and get dressed.

Julie: I want to speak to you. It's important.

Follavoine: It'll have to wait. It's nearly twelve. Chouilloux and his wife're coming to lunch and you look like an unfilled sack.

Julie: Chouilloux and his wife! I wouldn't give them house room.

Follavoine: Chouilloux could be worth two million francs to us.

Julie: You can have my interest in him for two centimes.

Follavoine: Just don't forget he's a powerful man to have on my side.

Julie: Who's more important. Chouilloux or Baby?

Follavoine: Chouilloux or Baby?

Julie: You have to think about it do you?! That's typical. Go on, tell me Chouilloux's more important. Tell me he's more important than your own son. Tell me!

Follavoine: Chouilloux . . . Baby . . . what's that got . . . Of course Baby's more important . . . Just because I have to be nice to . . . Of all the *fatuous* . . . Now let's calm down. Chouilloux'll be here any minute. He's coming to lunch so we can talk over some business.

Julie: Talk all you want.

Follavoine: You're not listening again! He'll be here any minute. Are you going to let him see you like that?

Julie: Like what?

Follavoine: *That!* That filthy bathrobe. That damn bucket and those, those, *stockings!*

Julie (*putting the bucket down in front of her*): So it's my stockings again. Is that all you can think about? (*she puts one foot on the bucket at a time and adjusts her stockings*) I suppose Chouilloux never saw stockings fall down before. I'm sure when Madame Chouilloux gets up in the morning she puts on an evening dress.

Follavoine: I don't know what his wife puts on. I'm pretty certain it isn't anything like you're wearing. Nobody wears what you're wearing when they invite people to lunch. Especially if it's people they've never met before.

11

Julie *starts looking through his papers again.*

Julie: Don't worry, you more than make up for me. Frankly, you're overdressed.

Follavoine: Overdressed?! I'm dressed as a gentleman should when he's receiving guests. What you looking for?!

Julie *(taking some elastic bands from a box)*: I've found them . . . *(she puts an elastic band around each leg to hold up the stockings)* Now perhaps you'll stop nagging me about my stockings.

Follavoine: Madame, those elastic bands're for my papers. They aren't damn garters!

Julie: They aren't garters because nobody uses them as garters. I'm using them as garters so they're garters.

Follavoine: God, what a nightmare!

Julie: So you're dressed as a gentleman should are you?! Eleven o'clock in the morning and you look as if you're going to a funeral. And all for that senile old fool Chouilloux. Damn cuckold.

Follavoine: Cuckold? Chouilloux? That's a terrible thing to say about anyone. Who told you a filthy story like that?

Julie: You did.

Follavoine: I did?

Julie: Yes. I don't even know the idiot.

Follavoine: All right. I told you. But I didn't know Chouilloux would turn out to be so important to me. Now I realize . . .

Julie: That his wife isn't cuckolding him.

Follavoine: Yes . . . No . . . I mean what difference does it make if she is or isn't. That's not why I'm inviting him to lunch. Why should it bother you what his wife does?

Julie: It doesn't bother me. She can have a dozen lovers and it wouldn't bother me. The only thing that bothers me is she's coming here to lunch. That woman, here in my house!

Follavoine: I couldn't very well invite him and not her.

Julie: And her lover, Horace Truchet. I suppose you invited him too?

Follavoine: Naturally. The three of them go everywhere together. If I didn't invite Truchet it would look suspicious. Even Chouilloux'd begin to wonder why.

Julie: That's lovely. So we've got all three of them. The whole unsavoury triangle. *(she picks up the bucket)* Nice friends to bring to your home. A fine example for Baby.

Follavoine: Baby? What does Baby know? He's only seven.

Julie: But next year he'll be eight.

Follavoine: And the year after that, nine. Meanwhile he's seven.

Julie: Your own child and you're not interested how he grows up. You don't care about his morals or his health, whether he's sick or well.

Follavoine: What do you mean sick or well?

Julie puts down the bucket, Stage Centre and moves across to Follavoine, who has sat down at his desk.

Julie: You don't listen do you? I've been trying to tell you all morning. Your son isn't feeling well. But every time I open my mouth to talk about Baby you bring up Chouilloux, Chouilloux, Chouilloux! Monsieur Cuckold Chouilloux!

Follavoine: What is it?! What about Baby?!

Julie: Oh, now you're interested.

She sits down on the bucket as if it were a stool.

Follavoine: Don't!

Julie: Don't what?

Follavoine: Not the wash-bucket! Find another place to sit.

Julie: I'm quite comfortable.

Follavoine: I don't care if you're comfortable, Madame! A bucket isn't to be sat on. Use a chair like any other human being.

Julie: Oh aren't we formal this morning. For Chouilloux's benefit no doubt.

Follavoine: I'm thinking of the carpet. You could knock it over and I don't want your dirty water on my carpet. What about Baby?

Julie: So you're ready to listen now are you?

Follavoine: Yes I'm ready.

Julie: No more interruptions about Chouilloux?

Follavoine: *Tell me!*

Julie: I'm worried, Baby hasn't gone this morning.

Follavoine: Gone?

Julie: Gone.

Follavoine: Gone where?

Julie: To the toilet. No bowel movement. Nothing.

13

Follavoine: Is that all?!

Julie: We've tried all morning. Four times he's sat there and tried. Not a sausage. Not even a little one this size. *(holds up her little finger)* Once I thought he had done it . . . false alarm. The pan was empty. He just sat there, poor darling, straining himself.

Follavoine: So he's a little constipated. What can I do?

Julie: A little constipated. What can I do?

Follavoine: Would you like me to go for him?

Julie: Baby's bursting and you think it's funny.

Follavoine: I don't think it's funny but I'm not going to start crying just because Baby's a little constipated.

Julie: It's serious, I was reading a book.

Follavoine: *You* were reading a book. A whole book?

Julie: Yes. History. It said an illegitimate son of Louis XVth almost died of a bad case of constipation when he was seven. Baby's seven and constipated.

Follavoine: But he's not illegitimate, stupid. There's no connection. If you're worried, give him some medicine to clear him out.

Julie: I don't need a fool to tell me that. I just don't know what medicine to give him.

Follavoine: Constipation—castor oil.

Julie *(getting up)*: Castor oil. Horrible. I can't stomach it.

Follavoine: You can't stomach it! You don't have it. It's for Baby.

Julie: Just talking about it makes me feel sick. I'll never take it. Why castor oil? We've got a full bottle of Dr Dacier's 'Quick Relief Liquid Laxative'. There's no reason to use castor oil just because *you* say so.

Follavoine: Because *I* say?! I only suggested . . .

Julie: I'll give him some of Dr Dacier's Liquid Laxative.

Follavoine: Fine. That's settled. I don't know why you bothered to ask me in the first place.

Julie: To find out what I should do.

Follavoine *(becóming absorbed in his papers)*: Now you know.

Julie: I suppose you think it's going to be fun getting him to take it? It always happens when I let his grandmother take him out.

14

Follavoine: What grandmother?

Julie: What grandmother? How many does he have? My mother of course.

Follavoine: Ah your mother.

Julie: Your mother! You always say 'Your mother' as if you were blaming me for it. I've told her not to, but every time she takes Baby out, she fills him with rubbish.

Follavoine: Well all grandmothers do.

Julie: You're always taking my mother's side against me. I tell her she shouldn't, you say 'well all grandmothers do'. Now I've got to pump Baby full of Dr Dacier's liquid.

Follavoine: It won't kill him.

Julie: It won't kill him! What a thing to say about your own son. He is yours you know.

Follavoine: I should hope so.

Julie: I'm not like Madame Chouilloux. I don't go around letting my 'cousin' do my husband's job for him. When I have a child, I have it with my husband!

Follavoine: Did I say you didn't?

Julie: It'd serve you right if he was someone else's. If I'd had him with . . . Louis XVth.

Follavoine: Louis the who?

Julie: XVth. He had illegitimate constipated children.

Follavoine *(sniggering)*: Oh, yes, Louis the XVth!

Julie: Go ahead and laugh, but you wait.

Follavoine: All right. We've decided Baby needs Dr Dacier's Liquid Laxative. So go give it to him.

Julie: It's not so easy. He won't like it.

Follavoine: He isn't meant to like it. Now, please, get dressed. Chouilloux'll be here and I haven't decided yet what I'm going to say to him.

He bends down to open a side drawer in his desk while **Julie** *crosses to the door Down Stage Right.*

Julie: It's awful stuff. Poor little thing.

Follavoine: Madame! *(he points to the bucket still in the middle of the room)* That! Please take it out. OUT.

Julie *(coming back)*: All you think of is that bucket and Chouilloux.

Follavoine: I've told you my study isn't the place for a bucket.

He carefully takes out a white chamber pot from the side of his desk. **Julie** *brays with laughter.*

Julie: That's good. Your study's too grand for my bucket but perfectly suitable for your smelly chamber-pot.

Follavoine: Chamber-pot? Did you say chamber-pot?

Julie: Yes. Unless that object in your hand is the latest fashion in hats.

Follavoine: It's a toiletry convenience. How can you compare your bucket with this. Your bucket's nothing, a common object. Whilst this . . . this toiletry convenience is . . .

Julie: A chamber-pot!

Follavoine: For you, but not for me . . . such purity of line and colour, every rift filled with . . . the result of hours of creative effort . . . it's a work of art, a thing of beauty, a . . .

Julie: A chamber-pot.

Follavoine: You think it's funny. But wait till it begins making us rich.

Julie: That chamber-pot?

Follavoine: With God's help. And Chouilloux's. I haven't told you before, I wanted it to be a surprise if everything works out. It's part of the Government's plan to improve conditions in the Army. They're trying to make our soldiers as comfortable as possible. One of the ideas is to stop the men catching cold.

Julie: What's that to do with your chamber-pot?

Follavoine: Instead of them going out in the middle of the night every time to answer nature's call, they're giving each man his own personally numbered chamber-pot. They're already taking bids to see what the new equipment should be made of, and who's going to make it. Naturally I'm bidding. Chouilloux's the Chairman of the Committee of Ways and Means examining all the different models. I've got the exclusive patent for unbreakable porcelain, so all I have to do is play up to him and the contract's mine!

Julie: Then what?

Follavoine: Then what? Then I'll be the exclusive supplier of chamber-pots to the Armies of France. And that's only the start. We could spread across the face of the globe: Europe, Africa, Asia and beyond. From Pole to Pole they'll all be using Follavoine chamber-pots. Today France, tomorrow the world!

Julie: The army's exclusive supplier of chamber-pots! But then everyone will know.

Follavoine: I'll see to that. Follavoine'll be a name they'll remember.

Julie: Never! It's revolting!

Follavoine: What do you mean revolting? It's no different from what I'm doing now. I sell chamber-pots every day of the week.

Julie: But you sell other things too. Cups, saucers, plates, those little figurines. But now you're going to *specialize*. And on those! No! Not even for the Government!

Follavoine: You're hysterical.

Julie: I'm not going through the rest of my life crowned with a chamber-pot! 'Who's that lady?' 'That's no lady, that's Madame Follavoine, the wife of the man who makes those chamber-pots.' 'Oh *that* Follavoine.'

Follavoine: For God's sake calm down. Whatever you do don't talk like that when Chouilloux's here.

Julie: Don't worry, I've nothing to say to that fool.

Follavoine: Good. But please don't ruin it. For my sake, for all our sake. When Chouilloux arrives, be polite.

Julie: I'm not in the habit of insulting my guests. I know how to act in society. My father once had the President to dinner.

Follavoine: That was before you were born.

Julie: What's that to do with it? He had him to dinner didn't he?

Follavoine (*guiding her towards the door, Down Stage Right*): He did. Now give Baby his medicine and get dressed. And take that bucket with you!

Julie (*picking up the bucket as she passes*): Don't keep telling me what to do.

    The doorbell rings.

Follavoine: It's Chouilloux. Hurry with the dressing. If he comes in and sees you like that?!

Julie (*in doorway*): What if he did?

Follavoine (*restraining himself*): I'd just rather he didn't . . . (*Julie exits slowly into the bedroom*) Slut! (*he takes a vase off*

17

a stand, puts the stand in a prominent position and places the chamber-pot on it in anticipation of **Chouilloux**'s *entrance; he waits expectantly; nothing happens)* Where is he? Rose! What is she doing? Rose, you will show Monsieur Chouilloux straight into my study won't you? Rose . . .

> **Rose** *knocks and comes in.*

Well, where is he? Who rang the doorbell?

Rose: A lady, Monsieur. She wanted you to pull out her teeth.

Follavoine: She wanted what?

Rose: Her teeth Monsieur. I told her the dentist was upstairs.

Follavoine: It's always happening. What're you staring at girl?

Rose: That chamber-pot.

Follavoine: It's not a chamber-pot. It's a piece of military equipment.

Rose: From the Azores Monsieur?

Follavoine: Will you go! *(Rose exits)* From the Azores. I'm surrounded by incompetents. *(he starts making calculations on a piece of paper)* Let's say the peace time strength of the army is what—three hundred thousand men? Yes, three hundred thousand. But there'll be new recruits coming in yearly. Ah, but when the old ones retire, they'll take their chamber-pots with them as mementoes of their Army days. It's a gold mine! If each pot costs . . .

> **Julie** *comes back in carrying the bucket and dressed exactly as before.*

Julie: Maximilien, come here a minute.

Follavoine: Can't you see I'm busy!

Julie: Maximilien! I'm asking you. Baby won't take his medicine.

Follavoine *(he looks up and reacts in horror)*: Ahhhh! You're still not dressed . . . and that, that, BUCKET!

Julie: I didn't have time to empty it.

Follavoine: Get that damned thing out out!

Julie: But Baby.

Follavoine: Get it OUT!

Julie *(plonking the bucket down in the middle of the room)*: I've had enough about my bucket. I'm not your maid. If you want it out, you take it out.

Follavoine: It's your dirty water, not mine.

Julie: It's yours! I give it to you free.

She crosses back to the door, Up Stage Right, **Follavoine** *goes after her with the bucket.*

Follavoine: Julie!

Julie: It's yours! *(she exits into the bedroom Down Stage Right)*

Follavoine: Get this filthy thing out . . .!

Rose *enters Up Stage Centre with* **Monsieur Chouilloux.**

Rose: Monsieur Chouilloux.

Chouilloux: Good morning.

Follavoine: Can't you see I'm talking, you idiot! *(he turns round suddenly and sees* **Chouilloux***)* Monsieur Chouilloux! Monsieur Chouilloux I didn't . . . *(to* **Rose***)* Why didn't you announce Monsieur Chouilloux? He should've been announced. Can't you do anything? *(***Rose** *exits Down Stage Right as* **Follavoine** *crosses with the bucket)* Please excuse her Monsieur.

Chouilloux: Am I early?

Follavoine: Not at all . . . I was just speaking with my wife . . . I didn't hear you ring.

Chouilloux: I did ring. And that pretty young maid let me in. After all, I haven't the ability to walk through walls, *ha-ha.*

Follavoine: No, *ha-ha.* Very good, very witty Monsieur, *ha-ha.*

Chouilloux: Yes, I always try to see the humorous.

Follavoine: Yes. Very good. Let me take your hat.

Chouilloux: Ah, yes.

Follavoine *takes* **Chouilloux**'s *hat and gives him the bucket in exchange. Seeing what he has done he quickly snatches it back, then in his confusion puts* **Chouilloux**'s *hat in the bucket and hangs the bucket on the hat stand.*

Follavoine: It's not mine . . . I mean my wife was here a minute ago . . . and she . . . Rose! Rose! I must apologise again Monsieur, especially at a time like this when I have the honour . . . Rose! The great honour . . .

Chouilloux: No, please

Follavoine: It *is* an honour Monsieur Chouilloux. Believe me.

Chouilloux: Too kind. Too kind.

Rose *(entering)*: You called Monsieur?

Follavoine: Yes. Madame Follavoine's bucket. Take it out please.

She sees the bucket on the hat stand and takes it down.

Rose: This isn't the place for it. I expect Madame'll say it's my fault . . .

She takes **Chouilloux's** *dripping hat from the bucket.* **Follavoine** *stares in horror and snatches it from her.*

Follavoine: You stupid girl. That's Monsieur Chouilloux's hat. *(he puts it back on the hat stand)* Go and tell Madame Follavoine Monsieur Chouilloux's here.

Rose: Yes, Monsieur.

She exits Stage Right with the bucket.

Chouilloux: Please don't trouble Madame Follavoine on my account.

Follavoine: No trouble. If I don't hurry her a little, she'll take all day. You know what women are.

Chouilloux: My wife's different. Every morning she's up at dawn and out she goes for a brisk walk. Can't get enough of it you know. Splendid exercise. I find it a little too strenuous. So she does it with her cousin.

Follavoine: So I've been told.

Chouilloux: I don't mind. Let Truchet have the pleasure.

Follavoine: Keep it in the family.

Chouilloux: That's right. Saves me the effort. Why should I be tired out every morning, eh? *(as they both laugh,* **Chouilloux** *sees the chamber-pot)* I see you've been working on our little business venture. That's the chamber-pot?

Follavoine: You recognise it?

Chouilloux: Immediately. It's good. Yes it's good.

Follavoine: Look at the full classical line. *(he taps the chamberpot with a pencil)* Listen to that tone . . . C sharp, clear as a bell. I've known men with the gift able to play a tune on it when they . . .

Chouilloux: Really. And it's made of unbreakable porcelain?

Follavoine: Absolutely unbreakable.

Chouilloux: You understand that's what especially attracted the Under-Secretary and me to your product. If it were just ordinary porcelain I don't think we'd be interested. You just look at it and it breaks.

Follavoine: Whereas this one, the Follavoine Special. Well it speaks for itself. It'll last a life-time. Here take it, feel it.

You're the expert.

Chouilloux: Oh no, no. I wouldn't say I'm an expert.

Follavoine: No false modesty, Monsieur. Just feel how light it is. Light yet durable.

Chouilloux *(he takes the pot from him, weighing it in his hand)*: Hhmm yes, like gossamer.

Follavoine: And how cool and smooth to the touch. It's a privilege to use a Follavoine Special. A privilege and a pleasure. It comes in white or any colour you choose. For the Army I thought perhaps stripes—blue, white, red. They'd be reminded of the flag they serve every time they used it. Perhaps embossed with the Cross of Lorraine.

Chouilloux: No. Too pretentious, wouldn't you say?

Follavoine: You're right. Too pretentious. Why waste Government money.

Chouilloux: We've time to think about colour and size later. *(he puts the pot back on the desk)* You know we've been looking at other designs too. The enamel chamber-pots look rather promising.

Follavoine: Enamel? Ooohh, I don't . . . well it's not for me to say.

Chouilloux: What is it Monsieur, speak out.

Follavoine: I'm not one to decry a rival product. The enamel chamber-pot has its advantages, no question, but frankly, they smell. Use them for a month and they start stinking. Nothing you can do, they stink. And then they turn yellow. Stain and stink that's the trouble with enamel chamber-pots. Marvellous except for that. And of course they spread disease. I've a nephew who got appendicitis from an enamel chamber-pot.

Chouilloux: How can anyone get appendicitis from an enamel chamber-pot?

Follavoine: With the youth of today it's easy. A few soldiers try out their new equipment. They brew up fresh coffee—the heat cracks the enamel—that's another thing against enamel, it cracks—a few chips fall into the coffee. They drink and *ahh ahhh*. You can imagine the rest can't you?

Chouilloux: No. I've never drunk coffee from a chamber-pot.

Follavoine: But you were in the Army.

Chouilloux: No. When I went for my medical the doctor said 'Can you see this?'. I said 'See what?'. That was the end of my military career. I've been with the War Office ever since.

Follavoine: And doing a marvellous job for your country Monsieur. Anyway, take my word for it, no enamel. Clay perhaps. Even rubber, if you must. But nothing's as good as porcelain in the long run. It's only drawback is it's too fragile, but we've taken care of that. Here let me show you. *(he puts the stand away then picks up the chamber-pot)* A demonstration. You'll see just how strong it is. *(he raises the pot high to throw it on the floor but stops)* No. There's a rug. That wouldn't prove anything. The wall . . . *(he is about to throw the pot at the wall but stops again)* No, that might cause damage and my wife . . . the desk. That's it, the desk. *(he pushes his papers to one side to clear one corner of his desk)* This should be satisfactory. Watch closely Monsieur. The Follavoine Special. *(he swings the pot above his head)* One . . . Two . . . Three . . .!

> He crashes the chamber-pot against the corner of his desk.
> It smashes into pieces, leaving him holding the pot handle. A
> long pause as the two men gaze at it in astonishment.

Chouilloux: It broke.

Follavoine: Hhmmmm . . .

Chouilloux *(looking at the pieces)*: No doubt about it.

Follavoine *(slowly)*: Yes . . . It broke . . . *(he puts the handle down quickly)* That's the first time. It never happens as a rule.

Chouilloux: Perhaps there was a flaw.

Follavoine: Of course. That's it, a flaw. It takes an expert like you to spot something as technical as that. I'm certain it's the exception that proves the rule. They never break. Well, perhaps one in a thousand.

Chouilloux: One in a thousand.

Follavoine: One in a thousand. I'll show you.

> He takes out a key, opens a cabinet on the left of the doors
> Up Stage Centre, to reveal rows of chamber-pots.

Pick any one you like, Monsieur. (**Chouilloux** *points to a pot*) Would you like to change your mind? (**Chouilloux** *shakes his head and* **Follavoine** *carries it over to the desk*) Now watch.

One . . . Two . . . *(he raises the pot and changes his mind)*
No. You do it, Monsieur.

Chouilloux: Me?

Follavoine: It's fairer. You'll get a better idea of the strength of the equipment.

Chouilloux *(raising the pot high)*: Very well . . .
One . . . Two . . . *(he hesitates)*

Follavoine: What is it?

Chouilloux: I've never done this before.

Follavoine: Don't be afraid. Nothing'll happen. One in a thousand.

Chouilloux: One in a thousand. One . . . Two . . . Three!
He smashes the pot down on the desk and it breaks into pieces. They survey the damage in silence

Follavoine: Hhmm . . .

Chouilloux: Two in a thousand.

Follavoine: Two in a thousand . . . I don't understand it must be the way we try and smash them. When my foreman tried it was all right.

Chouilloux: Perhaps the whole batch is flawed.

Follavoine: Of course. Why didn't I see that . . . *(he goes to the cabinet, takes another pot and smashes it to pieces on the side of the desk and so on with **Chouilloux**'s help smashes six more pots)* Flawed! All flawed! *(he goes to the second cabinet to the right of the doors, opens it and takes out another chamber-pot)* Now this is from a different batch. I think it'll prove my point. Watch . . . One . . . Two . . . *(as he swings the pot above his head, the bowl flies off and he is left with the handle in his hand)* Hhmm . . .

Chouilloux: Three in a thousand.

Follavoine: It proves what you said. It's not just one pot. Batches and batches of them are defective.

Chouilloux: They seem to be.

Follavoine: But I think you can appreciate the difference between ordinary breakable porcelain and . . .

Chouilloux: Unbreakable porcelain.

Follavoine: Yes. Still, something tells me I haven't completely convinced you.

Chouilloux: But you have. I understand perfectly. They're the same pots. Only instead of breaking, they don't.

Follavoine: That's it!

    Julie *enters Down Stage Right, dressed exactly as she was before.*

Julie: Maximilien, you must come and help me. I can't do anything with that child of yours.

Follavoine *(leaping at her, speaking low)*: What you doing?! You can't come in like that! Monsieur Chouilloux!

Julie: Monsieur Chouilloux can hang himself.

Chouilloux: What?

Follavoine: No! For God's sake! You stupid slut . . . Monsieur Chouilloux . . . my wife . . .

Chouilloux: Madame.

Julie: How are you? Please excuse me for coming in like this.

Chouilloux: Please Madame, think nothing of it. A beautiful woman looks lovely no matter what she wears.

Julie: Yes, yes. What's that mess on the floor?

Chouilloux: Unbreakable porcelain.

Follavoine: I was giving Monsieur Chouilloux a demonstration.

Julie: Well, who's going to clear it up?!

Follavoine: I was just about to when you came in.

Julie: Well it will have to be after you've dealt with baby. He's being difficult.

Follavoine: Madame, I'm discussing business with Monsieur Chouilloux. I've got more important things to do than giving your son a laxative.

Julie: More important things?! You heard that Monsieur. He's got more important things. That's a father speaking.

Chouilloux: Yes well . . .

Follavoine *(low)*: Will you get dressed! Look at yourself. Where's your pride?

Julie: Pride? How can you talk of my pride at a time like this?

Chouilloux: Is your child ill Madame?

Follavoine: It's nothing.

Julie: Nothing?! He hasn't gone this morning.

Chouilloux: Gone? Gone where?

Follavoine: That's exactly what I said. His bowels haven't gone.

Julie: And he says it's nothing!

Follavoine: All he needs is a tablespoon of Dr Dacier's Liquid to clear himself.

Julie: You just try giving it to him. That's why I asked you to come and help. I should've known better!

Follavoine: Good God Madame it's not that serious.

Chouilloux: No it isn't *that* serious. But you should never take something like that lightly.

Julie: You hear?

Follavoine: Well, Monsieur, of course you really know about such things. You think perhaps . . .

Chouilloux: It's possible . . . Madame Follavoine, is the child subject to 'er shall we say, constipation?

Julie: Yes, a little.

Chouilloux: Ah, then you must certainly watch his bowel movements. He could develop enteritis.

Julie: I knew it.

Chouilloux: I had enteritis for five years.

Julie (*looking towards the bedroom*): Oh. Poor darling.

Chouilloux: Thank you.

Julie: What?

Chouilloux: Five years of suffering. I caught it in 1888. In the war.

Julie: I don't remember a war in 1888.

Chouilloux: When I say 'in the war' I mean in the War Ministry. I'm an official there. I used to get terribly thirsty when I was young. I didn't care what kind of water I drank. I thought I was clever. I didn't listen to all that talk about germs and microbes. I drank it straight from the tap—why not? Then *bang*. I went down with enteritis. Just like that. I spent three years, off and on, in the clinic at Plombières trying to get rid of it.

Julie: You think Baby should go to Plombières?

Chouilloux: No. His case sounds rather like constipated enteritis. The Chatel-Guyon clinic would be better for him. You see my case was rather special . . . Shall we sit down?

Follavoine: Please Monsieur Chouilloux.

    They sit on the sofa.

Chouilloux: Yes, mine was a very special case. I had relaxed enteritis.

Follavoine: Relaxed? Good heavens! Relaxed?

Chouilloux: That's why Plombières was recommended. What a treatment they gave me.

Julie: What's the treatment like at Chatel-Guyon?

Chouilloux: At Chatel . . .? I don't know. I never went there. But at Plombières it was hard. Every morning at seven an internal rinse . . .

Julie: But at Chatel-Guyon, do they . . .?

Chouilloux: I don't know Madame. I never went there. Now after the rinse, a bath in the mineral springs. One whole hour. Then a massage . . .

Julie: Yes, yes, but . . .

Chouilloux: After the massage, lunch. Bland foods. Steamed fish, rice puddings.

Julie: But what about Chatel-Guyon?

Chouilloux: Chatel-Guyon? I never went there.

Follavoine: Chatel-Guyon?! Chatel-Guyon?! Monsieur Chouilloux keeps telling you he never went to Chatel-Guyon.

Chouilloux: No, I don't know about Chatel-Guyon.

Follavoine: He can only tell you his diet at Plombières.

Julie: I don't care about his diet at Plombières. Why should I care about the diet at Plombières when Baby needs the diet at Chatel-Guyon? You can see that can't you Monsieur?

Chouilloux: Yes I can but . . .

Julie: You might tell us how you went fishing off the Azores for bottle-nosed sharks. It would be interesting if you like that sort of thing, but it wouldn't have anything to do with Baby's enteritis.

Chouilloux: No quite, quite.

Julie (getting up): I'm very sorry, Monsieur, but I haven't time to listen to tittle tattle about Plombières or shark fishing. I have to give Baby his medicine.

Follavoine: Then give it to him!

Julie: Will you excuse me Monsieur Chouilloux?

Chouilloux: Certainly.

Julie: You won't come and help?

Follavoine: NO!

Julie: And you call yourself a father?! (she exits Down Stage Right)

Follavoine: I must apologise for my wife Monsieur Chouilloux.

She's under a strain.

Chouilloux: No, no your wife is charming Monsieur. Charming.

Follavoine: Charming? My wife? Well, yes, I suppose she can be, at times. I'm only sorry you haven't seen her at her best. When she actually dresses she's . . . and without those curlers and stockings and bathrobe . . . well, you can imagine. But she's worried about Baby at the moment.

Chouilloux: Oh I'm sure there's nothing seriously wrong.

Follavoine: That's what I told her. But you saw what happened when you mentioned that clinic at Chatel-Guyon? Now all she'll think about is Chatel-Guyon.

Chouilloux: She didn't seem to understand I've never been to Chatel-Guyon.

Follavoine (*laughing*): It happens so rarely that once she actually gets an idea into her head she doesn't like to lose it.

Chouilloux (*laughing*): 'What's the diet at Chatel-Guyon?' 'But I've never . . .'

As they both laugh loudly, **Julie** *enters Down Stage Right dragging* **Baby Toto** *with one hand and carrying a glass and a bottle of laxative in the other.*

Julie: Right! Just you wait and see what your father says. He's furious with you. Maximilien! I'm telling Baby you're furious with him and you're roaring with laughter.

Follavoine: What's the matter?

Julie: Make your son obey me. Give him his medicine (*she puts the bottle and glass on the table*) Show a little authority for once.

Follavoine: Excuse me a moment Monsieur.

Chouilloux: Of course.

Follavoine: Now young man, what's the meaning of this? Take your medicine.

Baby: I don't want to!

Julie: There! That's what I've had to put up with for the last half hour.

Chouilloux: Now is that the way for a big boy to talk?

He puts his hand on **Baby**'s *shoulder.* **Follavoine** *sees the child pull away petulantly.*

Follavoine: Say hello to the gentleman.

Baby: I don't want to!

Follavoine *(shaking the child)*: No-one cares what you want! Damn you!

Julie: Leave him alone! You're always maltreating the boy!

Follavoine: Maltreating?! Me?!

Julie: We'll have to find some way of making him take his medicine Monsieur Chouilloux. His tongue's all coated. Show the nice gentleman your tongue, Baby.

Chouilloux: Wait . . . *(he goes down on one knee in front of Baby)* Now then, let's see the trouble.

Julie: Go on, show him your tongue darling.

      Baby *sticks out his tongue.*

Chouilloux: It looks all right.

Julie: What about his breath? Go on, darling, say *aaah* in the gentleman's face.

Chouilloux *(reacting instinctively, protecting himself)*: Aaah.

Julie: Not you. Baby.

Chouilloux: Thank you but I . . .

Julie: You're not afraid of a child's breath surely? *(she pushes Baby's head nearer Chouilloux's face)* Go on, say *aaah* in his face.

Baby: AAAHHH!

Chouilloux *(scrambling up)*: No! It's not necessary. Now then young man, what's the trouble? Is this the way for a brave boy like you to behave? What's your name?

Follavoine: Tell the gentleman your name.

Baby: I don't want to.

Follavoine: His name's Toto.

Chouilloux: Toto? And how old are you, Toto? Six?

Julie: He's seven.

Chouilloux: Ah, so you're seven years old and your name's Toto. Now when a young man's seven and his name's Toto he shouldn't have any trouble taking his nice medicine, should he?

Baby: I don't want to.

Chouilloux: That's not good. If you won't take your medicine now how is it going to be when you grow up and you have to go to war?

Julie: War! What war?!

Baby: I don't want to go to war!

Chouilloux: If there's a war you'll have to go.

Baby: I don't want to. I'll run away to Switzerland.

Chouilloux: Switzerland?!

Julie: Mama's clever little angel!

Chouilloux: Switzerland, Monsieur! Why that's treason! Congratulations Follavoine, I suppose you've been filling the boy's head with those radical ideas?!

Follavoine: No. He thought it out by himself. I mean . . . You must never mention Switzerland again Toto. Never!

Julie (*crossing to the table and pouring medicine into the glass*): Leave the child alone. He doesn't have to worry about things like that at his age. He's Mama's darling and he's going to take his medicine like a big, strong man.

Baby: I don't want to!

Follavoine: You're going to obey me! Drink it!

Baby: I don't want to!

Chouilloux: When I was your age if my parents told me to do something, that was it. I obeyed.

    Baby *blows a loud raspberry at* **Chouilloux.**

Chouilloux: What? What?

Follavoine: Nothing! Nothing! Tummy upset.

Chouilloux: Oh yes . . .

Follavoine: Damn you, you little . . .!

Julie: Leave him alone.

Follavoine: You heard what he did?! (*blows a raspberry*)

Chouilloux: What?

Follavoine: Ah, there it is again.

Julie: He didn't mean it. You bully!

Follavoine: Right that's it. From now on leave me out of it.

Julie Never mind Toto. Now dear, take your medicine.

Baby: I don't want to!

Julie (*viciously at* **Follavoine**): See what happens when you interfere!

Follavoine: When I what . . .?!

Julie: Now Toto, if you drink your medicine like a good boy, Mama'll give you a peppermint.

Baby: Peppermint first.

Julie: No, afterwards.

Baby: Now! Now!

Julie: All right if you promise to take your medicine. Promise? *(Baby nods)* Your word of honour? *(Baby nods again)* I believe you. *(she turns to Follavoine who has buried his head in his hands)* Father! *(Follavoine doesn't answer)* Maximilien, box of peppermints. Box of peppermints!

Chouilloux: Box of peppermints.

Follavoine *(he opens a desk drawer and takes out the box)*: Box of peppermints. *(he gets up and gives them to Julie)* Please forgive me Monsieur Chouilloux for involving you in our little domestic troubles.

Chouilloux: Not at all. Most interesting for someone who's never had children.

Julie: Open wide angel. *(she puts the peppermint into Baby's mouth)* There . . . Is that nice? *(Baby nods)* Good. *(she holds out the glass of medicine)* Now drink Dr Dacier's lovely medicine.

Baby: I don't want to!

Julie: Toto!

Follavoine: There you see! You see! That little monster.

Julie: You promised. I gave you the peppermint.

Baby: I don't want to! I don't want to!

> *He runs across the room.* **Julie** *puts the glass down on the table and chases after him.*

Follavoine: I'll kill him!

Julie: Don't stand there shouting stupidities, help me. TOTO!

Follavoine: What? Just a minute ago you told me I was interfering. For God's sake no more! No more!

Julie: I should've known you'd be useless in a crisis.

Follavoine *(controlling himself)*: What . . . do . . . you . . . want?!

Julie: Nothing from you. I'm going to try something different. This is a fine time to pick to come to lunch!

> *She exits Down Stage Right, slamming the door.*

Chouilloux: Did you hear what your wife said?

Follavoine: Yes . . . time for a bit of lunch.

Chouilloux: Oh . . . time for . . . ah, yes.

Follavoine: That's bad of you, Toto. Breaking your word's a terrible thing, isn't it Monsieur Chouilloux.

Chouilloux: Yes. But I'd rather stay out of it if you don't mind.

Follavoine: Now Toto. Let's be sensible. You can't act like a baby anymore. Now if you take your medicine like a big boy, I've got a surprise for you.

Baby: What surprise?

Follavoine: I'll tell you where the Azores are.

Baby: I don't care.

Follavoine: So you don't care after all the trouble I had finding them. Well I'm going to tell you where they are whether you care or not. They're islands in the North Atlantic. They're a province of Portugal and the capital is Ponta Delgada.

Baby: What about Lake Como?

Follavoine: Lake Como?

Baby: Where's Lake Como, Daddy?

Follavoine: I just found out where the Azores are. But that is not good enough. Now you want Lake Como. Monsieur Chouilloux you wouldn't happen to know where Lake Como was or is?

Chouilloux: Lake Como? Italy. I swam there once, back in '77.

Follavoine: You did Monsieur. That's remarkable . . . You see Toto, you were looking for Lake Como. And here's a man who actually went swimming in it in '77. You wouldn't think so to look at him but he did. Now, take your medicine!

Baby: I don't want to!

Follavoine: *Arrrhh!*

Chouilloux: That boy has a mind of his own.

　　　Julie *returns, with another glass.*

Julie: Right here's another glass. *(she pours some medicine into it)* Now just to show you how easy it is, Daddy's going to drink some!

Follavoine: Daddy's what?!

Julie: Going to drink some medicine.

Follavoine: He is not!

Julie: It's for your own son.

Follavoine: My son?! Don't put all the blame on me. He's your son too.

Julie *(putting the glass on the desk)*: So I have to do all the dirty work again do I? It's always been like that, ever since he was born—and before. It wasn't easy carrying for nine months. Nine months in the depths of my womb.

Follavoine: Oh why didn't he stay there?

Baby: Mama, why did you carry me nine months? Why didn't Daddy?

Julie: Because he's your *father*. And he never does anything constructive. It was just one more job I had to do myself.

Follavoine: Really Monsieur Chouilloux, I ask you, is that something to tell a child?

Baby: You should've asked another man to carry me, Mama.

Follavoine: Asked another man. You see what you're teaching him?

Julie: There's no point in asking another man, Baby. They're all the same.

Baby: I won't be like that Mama.

Julie: No my angel. You have a heart.

Follavoine: Monsieur Chouilloux I must apologise again for subjecting you to this . . .

Chouilloux: Not at all. Charming. Children say such marvellous things. Out of the mouths of babes . . .

Julie: You see the difference between your father and your mother, Baby. *He* won't even take a laxative for you.

Baby: I don't want him to take it.

Follavoine: Ha! He's being more reasonable than you Madame.

Chouilloux: He doesn't want his Daddy to drink it does he?

Baby: No Monsieur, I want *you* to drink it!

Chouilloux: *Me!*

Follavoine: *Arrggx!*

Julie: You want him to drink it? Of course he'll drink it.

She takes the glass from the table and advances on **Chouilloux.** **Follavoine** *steps in front of her.*

Follavoine: For God's sake! No!

Julie *(brushing him aside)*: Keep away! Monsieur Chouilloux as a favour to me.

Chouilloux: *Madame!* That child is the worst . . . *aarrgg* (**Julie** *has put the glass forcibly to his lips and he has accidentally taken a mouthful),* Arrr!

Julie: Another little swallow Monsieur, it's not so bad. Come on now, be a man!

Chouilloux *(falling on sofa)*: Stay back woman!

Follavoine: Monsieur Chouilloux came for lunch not a laxative!

Julie: How can a grown man make so much fuss over a spoonful of Dr Dacier's Liquid Laxative.

Chouilloux: That's easy for you to say!

Julie: A man of your age, really! Now close your eyes and swallow. *(she puts the glass under his nose)*

Follavoine: JULIE.

Chouilloux: Not a laxative, Madame. With my intestines. I can't.

Follavoine: He can't.

Julie: Don't be ridiculous. What can half a glass do to your intestines?

Follavoine *(struggling to get the glass from her)*: Give me . . .!

Julie: And if I have to choose between your intestine and my Baby's health . . .

Follavoine: Will you . . .!

Chouilloux *(lurching up)*: You're not even sure if your child needs a laxative!

Julie: How can you say that? Right out loud in front of Baby. Now we'll never get him to take the filthy stuff.

Chouilloux: I'm sorry if I . . .

Julie: Sorry, sorry. You're always sorry!

Follavoine: Julie!

Chouilloux: I only thought . . .

Julie: You only thought! You didn't think, that's the trouble!

Follavoine: Julie!

Julie: Where did you find out about constipation?! At Plombières? You couldn't have. Any fool knows the diet's completely different there!

Chouilloux: All right, he *does* need a laxative.

Follavoine *(groaning)*: Julie . . .

Julie *(putting the glass down on the table)*: What business is it of yours anyway! Keep your nose out of other people's affairs. Do I say anything about your wife having an affair with her cousin? You cuckold! Everyone's laughing at you.

Chouilloux: *My wife . . . Cousin . . . Whaaaa . . .?*

Follavoine *(sobbing)*: It's not true!

Chouilloux *(clutching his throat)*: Cuckold . . . Water . . . Water . . .

He grabs the other glass of medicine left on the desk and

drinks it greedily before **Follavoine** *can stop him.* **Julie** *has seated herself unconcerned beside* **Baby** *on the sofa.*

Follavoine: Monsieur Chouilloux! Monsieur Chouilloux! Monsieur Chouilloux?

But **Chouilloux**'s *face contorts as his body twists and his arms flay out. Clutching his stomach, he looks around frantically. He desperately rushes over to the chamber-pots in the cabinet and snatches one but* **Follavoine** *grabs it.*

Follavoine: No! Outside. In the hall. Second door on the left. *(he guides him out Up Stage Centre)* Rose'll show you. Rose . . .! (**Chouilloux** *staggers into the hall and* **Follavoine** *puts the chamber-pot on his desk)* Thank you Madame! Thank you very much!

Julie: Baby has constipation. He should've minded his own business.

Follavoine: Telling him he was a laughing stock and a cuckold.

Julie: It's true.

Follavoine: What's that got to do with it!

Baby: Mama, what's a laughing stock?

Julie: You just saw one darling. That man's a laughing stock because his wife is having an affair with her cousin.

Follavoine: What are you saying?! In front of this monster! He's like a parrot.

Julie: If he'd drunk it when I asked him none of this would've come out.

Follavoine: It was a laxative woman! A *laxative*!

Julie: When someone invites you to their house, it's polite to accept what's offered. He comes here for the first time and immediately starts talking about his intestines. No breeding.

Follavoine: But you made him take a laxative! Now his bowels're loose and who knows what'll happen.

Julie: If his bowels're loose, that's his business. Nothing to do with me.

Follavoine *(suddenly collapsing)*: My God, what's going to happen to me? I've lost that contract . . . lost everything . . .

Julie: Contract? That's all you think about.

Follavoine: All down the pan with the rest . . . *(the doorbell rings)* That'll be Madame Chouilloux and Monsieur Truchet. I can't speak to them now! I'll see how Monsieur

Chouilloux's getting on. You deal with the others.

Julie: I don't even know them.

Follavoine: Don't worry, just be your usual charming self and I'm sure they won't stay long.

> *He staggers out Up Stage Centre. There are confused greetings from the hallway. The elegant* **Madame Chouilloux** *sweeps in with* **Monsieur Truchet.**

Madame Chouilloux: Ah, Madame Follavoine.

Julie: Madame Chouilloux.

Madame Chouilloux: I was afraid we might be early. *(she looks coolly at* **Julie***'s attire)* But I'm glad to see I was mistaken and you're all ready and waiting. Charming.

Julie: You must excuse me. I haven't been able to dress yet.

Madame Chouilloux: Please, Madame Follavoine. Don't stand on ceremony for us. May I introduce Monsieur Truchet, my cousin.

Truchet: Madame, I do hope we haven't put you out.

Julie: Not at all Monsieur.

> **Madame Chouilloux** *sees* **Baby.**

Madame Chouilloux: Oh is that your little girl? How adorable.

Julie: No . . . Yes . . . No, it's a boy.

Madame Chouilloux: Oh, at that age it's so hard to tell.

Truchet: Is your husband joining us?

Julie: Yes. He's just gone upstairs for a minute.

Baby: With a laughing stock.

Madame Chouilloux: What did he say?

Julie: He's with one of my husband's workers. From Dresden. Otto von Laffingstock.

Madame Chouilloux: What a delightfully quaint name.

> *They all laugh.* **Chouilloux** *comes storming in Up Stage Centre, followed by* **Follavoine.**

Follavoine: But I assure . . .

Chouilloux: Get away from me!

Madame Chouilloux: Ah, Gustave.

Chouilloux: Bitch!

Madame Chouilloux: What?

Follavoine: Oh God . . .

Chouilloux: Adulteress!

Madame Chouilloux: Me?!

35

Chouilloux *(pointing to* **Truchet***)*: And there. The worm in the apple! The snake in the garden! The faithless friend!

Truchet: Me?

Chouilloux: And here. The poor trusting husband! The blind fool! The laughing stock!

Madame Chouilloux: From Dresden?

Truchet: Who told you such lies?!

Chouilloux: Who told me? *(he points to* **Follavoine***)* He told me! *(points to* **Julie***)* She told me! *(he points to* **Baby***)* Even he told me! Everybody in this house told me!

Follavoine: It's not true Monsieur.

Madame Chouilloux: Now Gustave . . .

Chouilloux *(brushing her aside)*: Out of my sight harlot! You've seen the last of me. And as for your paramour. *(he bows formally to* **Truchet***)* Monsieur Truchet, we shall meet at dawn on the field of honour. At dawn! Hat! Hat!

    Follavoine *rushes to get* **Chouilloux***'s hat.* **Chouilloux** *grabs it from him and in the excitement puts his fist through the crown.*

Madame Chouilloux: Gustave, you can't believe this vile slander!

Truchet: Chouilloux, my dearest friend. On my honour as a gentleman . . .

Chouilloux: Enough! The rest is silence!

    He puts on his battered hat and exits Up Stage Centre, followed by his protesting wife and **Truchet**. **Truchet** *comes straight back in.*

Truchet: Now Monsieur, did you tell him that?

Follavoine: No! My wife.

Truchet: I see, hiding behind a woman, eh? You'll pay for this insult. *(he slaps him across the cheek)* Monsieur, you may choose your weapons. At dawn. Good day, Monsieur. *(he storms out)*

Julie: I hope you're satisfied with what you've done. I suppose I'll have to clean up this mess?! Who told you to invite those people to lunch? It's all your fault! *(she exits Down Stage Right)*

Follavoine: I'm ruined . . . Contract down the pan . . . I have to fight a duel at dawn . . . I might be killed . . . and it's my fault!

He lets out a scream of rage and, not realising what he is doing, staggers over to the table, picks up the remaining glass of medicine and swallows it in one gulp. A long pause as he slowly looks at the glass. Too late. His face is convulsed. He gasps and staggers Up Stage as **Baby** *rushes across and picks up the empty glass.* **Julie** *returns Stage Right with bucket and broom.*

Baby *(showing her the empty glass)*: Look Mama, I drank it! I drank all my medicine!

Julie: You drank it. You little angel! You see it wasn't very difficult was it?

Baby: No it was easy.

Follavoine, who has been stuck in the doorway clutching his stomach, staggers back to the hatstand and puts on his hat.

Follavoine: That's it, I've had enough. That's mine I think!

He crosses to his desk and snatches up the chamber-pot.

Julie: Baby's such a good boy. He's taken all his medicine.

Follavoine: Goodbye. I'm going.

Julie: Where to? The Azores?

Follavoine: Shit!

Follavoine *lashes out at her with the chamber-pot, misses and hits the edge of the desk instead. The chamber-pot does not break. He stares at it, bangs it against the desk again and again; then staggers out waving the unbroken chamber-pot and sobbing.*

Follavoine: Monsieur Chouilloux! Monsieur Chouilloux! Monsieur Chouilloux!

Sound of toilet being flushed.

CURTAIN

THE SINGER

by
Frank Wedekind

CHARACTERS

PAGE BOY
VALET
GERARDO
ISABEL
YOUNG WOMAN
HELEN
MÜLLER

A Berlin Hotel 1898

The Singer was first presented by James Verner at the Old Vic Theatre, London, on 11 October 1976, with the following cast:

Page Boy	Ashley Knight
Valet	Earl Robinson
Gerardo	John Stride
Isabel	Joan Morrow
Duhring	Leonard Rossiter
Young Woman	Allyson Rees
Helen	Dilys Laye
Müller	John Phillips

Directed by **Peter Barnes**
Designed by Michael Annals
Lighting by Leonard Tucker

THE SINGER

Gerardo *sings an aria from 'Tannhäuser'. Lights up on a pretentious hotel room. Large door Up Stage Centre to the corridor. Side door Down Stage Right to the bedroom. Curtain windows Stage Left. Opposite Stage Right, a grand piano and behind it a Japanese screen in front of a fireplace. A sofa nearby. Bouquets of flowers piled up on the chairs and piano.*

As a **Valet** *packs clothes into open trunks standing around, there is a knock on the door, Up Stage Centre. He crosses and opens it. A* **Page Boy** *enters, carrying three large bouquets and a batch of letters.*

Page Boy: For Herr Gerardo . . . There's a lady down in the lobby who wishes to know if Herr Gerardo is in.

Valet: No he isn't.

He takes the bouquets and letters. The **Page Boy** *exits as the* **Valet** *dumps the flowers on the chairs and sniffs a letter in a coloured envelope.*

Hmm . . . *(he sniffs another letter)* Hhmm . . . *(sniffing another)* That one too.

He puts the letters on a silver tray and resumes packing the clothes as **Gerardo** *enters, Stage Right, doing voice exercises.*

Gerardo: Haven't you finished packing yet?

Valet: Not quite, sir.

Gerardo: Hurry up then, I've got work to do before I leave. *(he looks inside one of the trunks)* What you doing? Don't you know how to fold a pair of trousers? *(he takes out the*

41

trousers) Look, this is the way to do it . . . *(he holds the trousers up)* If you hold them like this they fall straight, that's the secret . . . creases together, turnups in line . . . flick them over . . . So . . . Now they won't lose their shape.

He hands the neatly folded trousers to the Valet, *who puts them away.*

Valet: You're very professional, sir.

Gerardo: I always try to be.

Valet: Have you ever been a valet, sir?

Gerardo: I've been everything. Except an idler and a parasite. See if I've left anything in the bedroom.

As the Valet *exits Stage Right,* Gerardo *picks up the letters from the tray, sniffs one, grimaces and tears it open whilst still doing his voice exercises.*

Gerardo *(reading)*: 'The Greatest Singer in the World . . .' *(he nods in agreement)* Hhm yes . . . 'I belong to you. You are my god . . . take me . . . Make me happy the rest of my life . . . I long . . . etc . . . etc.'

He screws up the letter and throws it into the waste paper basket, opens another and reads

'My Dearest . . .' Impudence . . .! 'Take pity on me . . . I long to . . .' My God!

He whistles incredulously then screws up the letter and throws it and the rest of the unopened envelopes into the wastepaper basket.

I'm supposed to sing *Tristan* in Brussels tomorrow and I can't remember a note! *(takes out his watch)* Three thirty. Forty-five minutes. *(there is a knock on the door)* Yes!

The Page Boy *enters with a huge bottle of champagne*

Page Boy: I was told to put this in Herr Gerardo's room.

Gerardo: Over there. If there's someone downstairs wanting to come up, I'm not in.

He tips the Page Boy.

Page Boy: Thank you sir.

He exits. Gerardo *looks at the huge bottle.*

Gerardo: It's monstrous. What am I supposed to do with it?

He looks at the card attached and grimaces as the Valet *comes back from the bedroom, Stage Right*

Valet: There's nothing more, sir. *(he closes the trunks)*

Gerardo: I'm at home to no-one. I'm out. You haven't seen me.

Valet: You may depend on me, sir.

Gerardo: To no-one. No-one!

Valet: I understand sir. I'll see the trunks are taken down at once.

Gerardo *(giving him a large tip)*: To no-one!

Valet: Thank you, sir. No-one. Absolutely no-one. I haven't seen you. No-one has seen you. No-One.

He exits Up Stage. **Gerardo** *looks at his watch*

Gerardo: About forty minutes left . . .

He throws the flowers on the piano on the floor, finds the piano arrangement of 'Tristan and Isolde' under them and walks up and down practising scales.

Doh-Ray-Me-Me-Me . . . *(he repeats the lyric)* 'Isolde! Beloved! Art thou mine? Once more my own? May I embrace thee?' *(he stops, clears his throat, strikes a note on the piano)* 'Isolde! Beloved! Art thou mine? Once . . .' *(he stops, clears his throat)* The air's hellish in here. 'Isolde! Beloved!' It's like a dead weight on my chest. I'm suffocating.

He crosses to the curtains Stage Left, and pulls them open to reveal **Isabel Coeurne** *hiding behind them; he reacts with a groan of despair.* **Isabel** *is young and carries a bouquet of red roses.*

Isabel: Don't send me away, please.

Gerardo: Why not? I didn't ask you to come here. Look, I'm sorry, but I have to sing tomorrow night and I've only got half-an-hour to myself to practise. I've given strict orders not to be disturbed. I'm sure you understand. You must go.

Isabel: I heard you sing *Tannhäuser* last night and just came to give you these roses.

She thrusts the roses at him. He takes them with a sigh.

Gerardo: Thank you and goodbye.

Isabel: And myself. I hope I said it right?

Gerardo: Who are you?

Isabel: Isabel Coeurne. Miss Isabel Coeurne.

Gerardo: Let us have a little talk, Miss Coeurne. *(he sits her in a chair and stands over her)* I think you need it. Now, just because I'm an artist . . . How old're you Miss Coeurne?

Isabel: Twenty-two.

Gerardo: A lie. You're making the supreme sacrifice of saying you're older because you think I'll find you more attractive. All in vain my child. You're just being silly. And my being an artist doesn't mean I have to waste time educating you.

Isabel: I thought German men liked girls to be silly.

Gerardo: I'm not German.

Isabel: Then I won't be silly.

Gerardo: And I won't play nurse-maid to a child. *(looking at her low-cut dress)* Though you're hardly a child are you?

Isabel: Not now.

Gerardo: No . . . Look, young lady, there's so much else you can do—lawn tennis, skating, bicycling, swimming, riding, dancing, mountaineering with your friends. All very healthy and energetic activities. Why do you have to come to me?

Isabel: Because I hate all that. It's so boring.

Gerardo *(leans over her for a moment)*: True. I always found outdoor entertainments boring. I wanted something else from life . . . *(he recovers)* But I'm thirty-eight—thirty-six years old; it's natural. In a couple of years I'm certain, something more satisfying'll turn up for you. Then you won't have to sneak into the room of a man you don't know—who nobody really knows and hide behind curtains. *(Isabel starts to sob)* There now. I do appreciate the sincerity of your feeling . . . and the roses. Thank you for the roses. *(he sits and presses her hand)* Will that satisfy you for now?

Isabel: I never thought of men until I saw you on stage yesterday as Tannhäuser. I promise you . . .

Gerardo: Don't promise. You'd be sorry for it. I'm speaking to you like a father, a loving father. Be thankful I'm not the sort of artist who'd take advantage of your indiscretion.

Isabel: Am I so hideous?

Gerardo: Hideous? Why you're young, beautiful . . . No, I haven't the time. *(he gets up)* I'm the ugly one. Yet wherever I go women keep popping up, throwing themselves at me. Even when I've only got a few moments to catch a train. I have to sing *Tristan* tomorrow night! Just because I'm a singer, it doesn't mean I have to spend time telling you you're beautiful. I'm too busy.

Isabel: You might not tell me, but you could think it.

Gerardo: Could I? Maybe . . . Young lady, I don't like hurting people! It's a failing of mine. You've sacrificed your pride to come here to throw yourself at me. I'm flattered. Really flattered. But you must be reasonable. At least two hundred—three hundred—eager young girls like you heard me sing *Tannhäuser* last night. Suppose they all turned up here offering themselves, expecting me to do for them, what you expect me to do for you? What would happen to my voice? After making three hundred happy. Think of it. Mine's a delicate instrument. I have to treat it with extreme care. *(Isabel sobs; he sits on the arm of the chair and comforts her)* Don't cry. You heard me sing last night. Be grateful for that. No sequels please. *(he gets up)* It's not my fault you've fallen in love with me is it? It's my manager! I told him about my costume. But he insisted. The breeches're too tight and the shirt's too open at the neck. You can see the hairs on my chest when I sing. It's sheer provocation, I told him. He wouldn't listen. There's more to opera than mere singing. Now be a good girl and go. I've only a few minutes and I must practise.

Isabel *(rising and going close to him)*: I can't imagine another girl acting like me. At least not . . .

Gerardo *(trying to manoeuvre her to the door Up Stage)*: My valet had been guarding the lobby like he's supposed to, not . . .

Isabel: Not if she's as respectable as I am!

> **Gerardo** *gestures to the flowers on the piano.*

Gerardo: Look at those flowers. Let them be a warning to you if you should ever be tempted to fall in love with an artist again. See how fresh they are now. I just let them fade or give them to the porter. And those letters. From unknown admirers like yourself. Into the waste basket with them.

Isabel: I won't hide behind the curtains again.

Gerardo: Good. Now you must leave. *(looks at his watch)* My train goes in twenty-five minutes. I have to practise.

Isabel: I won't do it again.

Gerardo: What more do you want?

Isabel: A kiss.

Gerardo: From me, child?

45

Isabel: Yes.

Gerardo: You're desecrating art with that suggestion. People don't pay to see me for that. When you're older you'll come to respect the chaste goddess Athena to whom I devote my life and my labour. Do you understand?

Isabel: No.

Gerardo: I thought somehow you wouldn't . . . You're so young, so beautiful. And there's just time.

He looks quickly at his watch, grabs her hand and disappears with her into the bedroom Down Stage Right. There is a scream and **Isabel** *rushes back out sobbing with fright.* **Gerardo** *appears in the doorway frustrated.*

Isabel: I'm too young.

Gerardo: You can have a photograph of me . . .

Isabel: Signed?

Gerardo: If you'll give me your word you'll go.

Isabel: Yes.

Gerardo *(crossing to the table he takes a photograph from a pile and signs it)*: Interest yourself in the opera rather than the singers. You'll find that a deeper pleasure in the end. Fall in love with the music not with me. Study the librettos. Learn to feel each and every marvellous leitmotiv. It will keep you from committing further indiscretions.

He hands her his photograph. She seizes it, kisses it and rushes out. He briskly rings for the **Valet.** **Isabel** *reappears in the doorway, gives him the original bunch of flowers, which she still has in her hands, and exits. He throws the flowers into the waste paper basket and goes back to the piano. Picking up the piano arrangement he starts practising again.*

Gerardo: 'Isolde! Beloved! Art thou mine? Once more my own . . .?' *(there is a knock on the door)* Come in!

The **Valet** *enters, Up Stage Centre.*

Valet: You rang sir?

Gerardo: Are you standing on guard in the lobby?

Valet: Not at the moment, sir.

Gerardo: I can see that you idiot. Just make sure no-one is let up to see me. No-one!

Valet: No-one. Three ladies downstairs are asking about you, sir.

Gerardo: No-one! I said no-one!

Valet: No-one, sir. And there's another batch of letters.

He's about to hand them to **Gerardo** *who points to the waste paper basket. The* **Valet** *drops the letters into it.*

Gerardo: You know my orders.

Valet: No-one, sir.

Gerardo: No matter how much they try and bribe you. I'll double it.

Valet: NO-ONE, Sir! *(he exits Up Stage Centre)*

Gerardo: 'Isolde! Beloved! Art thou . . .' I should've thought women would've got tired of chasing me. But then there are so many women in the world and only one Gerardo. We all have our cross to bear . . . 'Isolde! Beloved! Art thou mine . . .?'

As he crosses to the piano and strikes a note, **Professor Duhring** *bursts in Up Stage Centre dressed in a black frock coat and silk hat; he carries an opera score under his arm.*

Duhring: Herr Gerardo!

Gerardo: Ah! How did you get in?!

Duhring: I've been waiting for two hours to see you.

Gerardo: Er, you're . . .?

Duhring: I've been standing outside in the rain for two hours! So I came up! What else do you expect me to do?!

Gerardo: Sir, I haven't time to . . .

Duhring: I shan't play you the whole opera.

Gerardo: The whole *what?*

Duhring: The whole opera.

Gerardo: Opera?! I haven't the time . . .

Duhring: *You* haven't the time?! What about me?! You're a success still in your thirties and you haven't the time?! I'm only asking you to listen to your own part in the opera. You must've time for that!

Gerardo: I don't, I'm singing *Tristan* to-morrow. I've got to practise.

Duhring *(falling on his knees)*: Please Herr Gerardo! Look, Look I'm on my knees begging you. *(he clutches at* **Gerardo's** *legs)* Begging you! I'm an old man whose whole life has been devoted to his art.

Gerardo tries to move away, **Duhring** *clings to his leg and is pulled across the room.*

His art! His glorious art! You're a young man carried to the heights on the wings of song. I know what you're going to say. You're going to say, let the Goddess Fortuna find you, don't search her out. That's what you're going to say isn't it?

Gerardo *(disentangling himself)*: No.

Duhring: I can't, I can't. I thought of nothing else for fifty years but success, recognition. Recognition for what's in me, my gift. One has hopes at first, then one turns cynical, then bitter. I tried to get there by scheming, but I soon returned to the stony path of artistic integrity. None of it's for ambition's sake, you understand? One simply can't help it. We're cursed. Cursed! We suffer. Suffer! Yet this life-long agony is also our pleasure. Pleasure, I say, pleasure! We whom art has enthralled, rebel against her cruelties as little as a lovesick boy against his seductress or a dog against the master who whips him.

Gerardo: Oh God.

Duhring: Let me tell you, sir, the tyrants of antiquity who had their slaves tortured for fun were children, innocent little angels, compared with the Supreme Being who was supposed to have created those tyrants in His own image. Yes, yes?

Gerardo: What're you talking about?! I don't understand a word . . .

Duhring: You don't understand?! You don't understand?! No, you haven't time to understand. Fifty years of waiting, that's what you can't understand. Of course you can't understand. Success can't understand failure. Fortune's favoured you, given me ashes. Ashes! Now I'm too old to take my own life. The proper time to commit suicide is twenty-five. But I missed my opportunity. Now my hand shakes too much. I have to live out the rest of my life. Live it out! Live it out! I had to wait outside in the rain for two hours before I could slip past your valet. That's what a man of my years is driven to. That's what I have to do just to see a man who's young enough to be my grandson! Please, you must listen. Listen, listen. It'll be to your advantage as well as mine. I've called every day, but you've either been rehearsing or had visitors. All those women. Fortune's smiled there too. If you leave now it'll mean you've let a poor old man stand in the gutter for a week for nothing. It's so easy for you. All it'll cost is a single word, 'Yes.' 'Yes I will sing *Hermann.*' One word from you and my opera'll be performed. Then you'll thank me for my persistence. You will. Oh, you sing Siegfried, but there isn't anything in your repertoire to equal the part I've written for you in *Hermann.* Not for a singer of your resources. Don't thank me, you deserve it. And when the opera's a success, the applause, the applause'll draw me out, draw me out of my obscurity. I'll have the opportunity to give the world what it could've had long ago if it hadn't cast me out as a leper, as a leper, sir! Damn them! I shall expect no material gain from it. I've struggled years, but not for money. That's yours . . .

Gerardo, *who has given up trying to stop* **Duhring,** *is leaning, defeated against the mantelpiece when he notices something. He goes behind the Chinese screen in front of the fireplace and pulls out another* **Young Woman** *who has been hiding behind it. Holding her at arm's length by the collar, he marches her Up Stage and out of the room.* **Duhring** *has not stopped talking all the way through the incident.*

Maybe one good opera every ten years survives. Well, mine's a good one. It'll make money too. I can show you letters from Liszt, Wagner, Rubinstein, yes those men look up to me as their superior! Superior! So why aren't I performed? Because I won't sell myself. I won't shout in the market-place. No, sir, I'm like a great beauty who forgets to get married. You know our theatres. Fortresses. Armour-plated against the true artist. They'd rather dig up ten corpses than admit a single new living composer. Give me a hand up over the ramparts, sir. You're inside at thirty, I'm outside at seventy. Just a word so I can stop battering my head against steel and stone. If success hasn't killed off all traces of sympathy for a fellow-artist, you won't say no.

Gerardo: Leave your score with me. I'll play it through and let you know in a week what I think.

Duhring: No thank you! I'm too long in the tooth for that! I know your sort of week. I've had those weeks before. Those seven days'll take so long I'll be dead by the end of them. Five years ago I saw the manager of the Royal

Theatre—Count Zedlitz . . . 'What've you got for me, professor?' 'An opera your Excellency'. 'Ah, a new opera! Splendid! Splendid!' 'No your Excellency, it's not new. It's an old opera. Thirteen years old . . .' Not this one, Herr Gerardo. It was my *Maria de Medicis*. You've heard of it? No. Brilliant piece. Brilliant . . . 'Thirteen years, professor! But why didn't you let us have it then? We're always hunting for new work.' 'Your Excellency, I submitted this opera to your predecessor, Count Tounay thirteen years ago. I had to go to his office myself, three years later to get it back. They hadn't even opened the evelope.' 'Dreadful, dreadful, professor. Tounay was like that. Slack. Give it to me and I'll give you an answer in a week. One week!' So he takes my *Maria de Medicis*, and claps it into a drawer. And that's where it still is today, if the mice haven't got to it. But I was naive then. I went home and told my Gretchen. 'Gretchen, Gretchen, they need a new opera, mine's practically accepted.' She died a year later, still waiting. Dead! The only person left who knew me when I first started writing that piece.

Gerardo: I feel for you but . . .

Duhring: That's where it's lying now. Mice nibble the corners!

Gerardo: Perhaps you're still too naive. I doubt if I can help you.

Duhring: I knew it! So you can stand there and see an old man drag himself along in the gutter whilst you take the golden road to fame and fortune. Tomorrow you could be on your knees in front of me! Tomorrow you could be boasting you knew me once! Now you only hear the agonized cries of a creative artist in torment. Please, in your greed for gold you won't take half-an-hour to rid me of the chains that pull me down.

Gerardo (*slumping defeated into a chair*): Play, maestro, play!

Duhring (*he goes to the piano, opens the score and strikes two chords*): 'Er no, that's not the way it reads. I have to get back into it . . . (*he dramatically strikes three chords*) That's the overture. (*he turns several pages*) I won't detain you with that. Now here comes the first scene. Right . . . (*he strikes two chords*) You stand at the deathbed of your father. Now we see . . . Wait, just let me get my bearings. Right . . . (*he*

50

plays a confused orchestration and sings in a grating voice) 'Alas, now death comes to the castle. As it rageth in our humble huts. It moweth down great and small . . .' No, sorry, that's the chorus. I thought of playing it to you because it's so good. But that gives you a taste of it. Now comes your turn. *(he resumes the accompaniment and hoarse singing)* 'My life unto this fatal hour. Was dim and grey like winter's dawn. Tortured by devils, I roamed abroad. My eyes are dry. Oh, let me kiss again thy hoary hairs! . . . Well, have you ever heard anything like that before?

Gerardo *(low)*: Not emanating from a human throat.

Duhring: All those young, anaemic, clod-hopping eighteen-year-old, so-called geniuses. Burned out by the time they're twenty! Second-raters! They get it all out of books, imitating art not life. Music for musicians instead of yearning humanity. Blind! Blind! They're all senile, even the youngest. *(he suddenly grabs* **Gerardo's** *arm)* Do you know how I judge a man's creative gifts?

Gerardo *(trying to pull away)*: No!

Duhring *lets go of* **Gerardo**, *then puts his fingers on his own left wrist and feels his pulse.*

Duhring: I take hold of him here. Right here. If I can't feel anything then I know! Please, you must let me continue playing, we're wasting time. *(he turns over more papers of the score)* I won't go through the whole monologue.

Gerardo: Good.

Duhring: You haven't time, so you say. Now here, Scene Three, end of Act One. That's where the farm labourer's child, who's grown up with you in the castle, suddenly enters. Listen to this—it's after you've left your mother, a great lady. *(singing)* 'Demon, who art thou? Demon? May one enter here . . .?' You understand those words are his mother's. *(continues singing)* 'Barbette! Yes, it is I—or me'. 'Is your father dead?' 'There he lies! Full often didst he stroke my curls. He was always kind to me when we met. Alas, this is death. His eyes are closed . . .' Now tell me, isn't that music? Isn't that music?

Gerardo: Possibly.

Duhring *(striking two chords)*: It must be better than *The*

51

Trumpeter of Sackinger.

Gerardo *(getting up)*: Your self-confidence compels me to be candid. I can't help you.

Duhring: Are you saying my music's old-fashioned?!

Gerardo: I'm a Wagner singer, sir, not a music critic. If you want to see your opera performed, you must go to those who're paid to know if it's good or bad. Nobody cares about my judgement.

Duhring: My dear Herr Gerardo, I don't care about your judgement either. I may be naive, but I think I know what to expect from the judgement of a *tenor!* I'm simply playing this opera to you to make you say, 'I'll sing *Hermann!*' 'I'll sing *Hermann.*'

Gerardo: You don't understand. I have iron-bound contracts. You can stand in the gutter for a month if you like. But if I did it I'd be ruined. I'm a slave, you've been a free man all your life. You complain about the market-place. Why don't you come down and join us?!

Duhring: All that haggling over money, contracts. The shouting, cheating, twisting, double dealing. I've tried, I've tried.

Gerardo: And you've failed. Perhaps it's the same with you as a composer.

Duhring: I'm not a pedlar. But I *am* a composer. A composer!

Gerardo: You mean by that you've devoted the last ounce of your strength to writing your operas.

Duhring: Absolutely. The last ounce of strength.

Gerardo: And you haven't any left to get them performed.

Duhring: Absolutely.

Gerardo: The composers I know do exactly the opposite. They slap their operas down on paper any old way they can and save their strength for getting them performed.

Duhring: I despise that kind of composer.

Gerardo: I'm sure it's mutual. But these composers are known. One must be someone. Name me a single famous man who's unknown!

Duhring: Er . . .

Gerardo: If you fail as a composer you do something else, that's all. It's no tragedy. Do you know what I was before I was discovered? A paper-hanger's apprentice. And a damn good one. Papered hundreds of walls in my time. It's an art. You have to have the touch. I was happy. I don't hide my humble beginnings. But just imagine when I was paper-hanging if I'd've taken it into my head to become a Wagner singer. You know what they'd've done to me?

Duhring: Put you into an asylum.

Gerardo: And quick. And rightly. A healthy man does what he's successful at, if he fails, he does something else. I was discovered. I found I was a better singer than paper-hanger, so I did that. You speak of the judgement of your friends. It doesn't take much to get their praises. It costs them nothing. There's no money involved. Since I was fifteen, I've been paid for every job I've done. I think it demeaning to do something for nothing. Fifty years of fruitless struggle. That's not heroic, it's blind stupidity.

Duhring: Blasphemy! How can you say that whilst you're actually holding my opera?! *(he snatches back his score)* You forget I'm not doing it all for my sake, I'm doing it for art. *Our* art!

Gerardo: You overestimate it.

Duhring: There's nothing higher in life.

Gerardo: It's in a lot of people's interest to make everyone think so. Art is one of the luxuries of the bourgeoisie. They outbid each other to get their hands on a piece. Yet when I'm standing on stage singing *'Walküre'* I know not a single person in the audience is paying the slightest attention to what the composer is actually saying. If they did, they'd get up and leave in disgust. That's what they actually did when the work was first performed. And that's art! That's what you've sacrificed fifty years of your life for. Artists only have one duty, to give themselves to the paying public on one pretext or another. And because we do it for money, they don't know whether to idolize or despise us. Go and find out how many went to the theatre yesterday to actually hear me sing and how many to come and gawp at the fairground freak. Do you know what the public really wants from art and artists? It's the excuse to shout bravos, throw roses on the stage. To have something to talk about, to see and be seen, to say *Oooh* and *Ahh*, to shout 'encore! encore!'. That's what the public wants from art and I give it to them. They pay me a fortune, but I make money circulate. I provide a living for hordes of cabmen, waiters, milliners, florists, hotel managers and musicians. A lady is robbed of her purse, a gentleman goes insane during a performance, a child is trampled to death at the box office. It's still good business for doctors, lawyers . . . *(he has a fit of coughing, seizes a throat spray from the table and sprays his throat)* God, how am I going to sing *Tristan* tomorrow in this condition? I'm not telling you all this out of vanity, but to cure you of your delusions about art and life. The standards by which a man's importance in this world is judged is the world's standard, not some arbitrary set of conditions created by you after fifty years of morbid brooding. How can a man be so stubborn? Can't you see. Your dreams are impossible!

Duhring: I must play you the first scene of the Second Act before I go. It takes place in a park just like that picture, *'Embarquement pour Cythere . . .'*

Gerardo: No! How many times do I have to tell you. Even if I wanted to sing *Hermann* I couldn't. You're an unknown composer.

    Duhring *rises with great dignity and starts packing up his score.*

Duhring: I'm afraid, sir, you misjudge me. I'm not quite as unknown to the rest of the world as I am to you. Wagner often mentions me in his writings. And let me tell you, if I were to die today, I know my works would be performed tomorrow. My Berlin publisher writes to me every day. 'To be a success, all you have to do, is die'. 'Why don't you?' he keeps asking.

Gerardo: Well, since Wagner's death, no-one wants new operas. Offer them new music, you'll have the managers, the singers and the public against you from the start. If you want your stuff performed, just write what's in fashion, copy. Steal bits from Wagner. It's the old stuff they want. Anyway why should I have the sweat of learning new music when I've suffered so much learning the old?

Duhring: Steal? Did you say steal? I'm too far gone to learn to steal. That's the kind of thing one has to start young.

Gerardo: I hope I haven't offended . . . If you'd permit me . . . Your life's hard . . . it so happens I received five hundred marks more than I . . .

Duhring: Never! Don't finish what you were about to say. Money?! How dare you, sir?! *(he shudders) Money . . .!* I came to ask you to listen to my opera and not to beg for money! Money! *(clasping his score tightly)* I love my child too much to have it soiled by money! No indeed, sir. Money! How could you?! MONEY! MONEY! *(He exits Up Stage Centre)*

Gerardo *(calling after him):* Nice to have met you Herr . . . Professor . . . hmm . . . Money . . . yes . . . it's only money. Why am I working so hard? Two more years like this and I'll be finished . . . *(suddenly looks at his watch, jumps up and starts practising again)* 'Isolde! Beloved! Art thou mine? Once more my own . . .'

    Helen, *a strikingly handsome woman bursts in Up Stage Centre.*

Helen: I suppose you placed that idiot in the lobby to stop me from seeing you.

Gerardo: Helen.

Helen: You knew I was coming didn't you?

    The **Valet** *appears in the open doorway, feeling his jaw.*

Valet: I did my best sir, but this lady . . .

Helen: I hit him.

Gerardo *(to* **Valet***):* Yes, thank you. I'll be all right.

    The **Valet** *exits.*

Helen *(laying her muff on the chair):* Oscar, I can no longer live without you. Either you take me with you or I shall kill myself.

Gerardo: Helen.

Helen: I shall kill myself, do you hear?! You cut my throat if you go. I can't live through another day like yesterday without seeing you. A whole day. I can't! I'm not strong enough. *(she flings herself on* **Gerardo** *and clings to him)* Please, Oscar, take me with you! Please! I'm pleading for my life!

Gerardo *(trying to disentangle himself):* It's impossible.

Helen: Impossible?! How can you say it's impossible?! The only

55

thing that's impossible is for you to leave me without killing me. I mean it. If I can't have you I'll die. Take me with you. Even if it's only for a short time, I don't care. Only take me!

Gerardo: Helen. I give you my word of honour I can't. Word of honour.

Helen: If you won't take me, then take the consequences, Oscar. My life is dear to me, but we're bound together. Take me or see me bleed!

Gerardo *manages to pull her off him.*

Gerardo: Do you remember what I told you the very first day in this very room?

Helen: What's the good of all that now?

Gerardo: That there could be no real sentiment between us. No love in our affair.

Helen: I didn't know you then. I didn't know what a man could be like 'till I met you. You knew it'd come to this so right at the start you got me to promise things to avoid a scene when you left. That was cruel, Oscar. Besides, you knew I'd've promised you anything then, if you'd asked. That promise means my death.

Gerardo: I can't take you.

Helen: I knew you'd say that! You always say that to them! I'm no better than the others am I? One of a hundred women. A million. But Oscar I'm different. I'm sick with love, Oscar. Nearer to death than life. Only you can save me. And without sacrificing anything. Why won't you save me Oscar?

Gerardo: Because my contract forbids me to marry or travel around with a woman.

Helen: You're not allowed to . . .?

Gerardo: Marry until my contract expires.

Helen: And you're not allowed to . . .?

Gerardo: Travel around with a woman.

Helen: Why? Who cares?

Gerardo: My manager.

Helen: What business is it of his?

Gerardo: It *is* his business.

Helen: Is it because it might affect your voice?

Gerardo: Yes.

Helen: That's idiotic. Does it affect your voice? Women I mean?

Gerardo: It does not.

Helen: Does your manager believe such nonsemse?

Gerardo: No, but owners of the theatres do. They provide the money.

Helen: How can an intelligent man sign such a contract?

Gerardo: My rights as an intelligent man don't come into it. I'm just an artist, who wants to be paid.

Helen: You're a great artist. (*she throws off her cloak*) All that makes me appear contemptible now is due to that. You're the only man who's ever made me feel his utter superiority. I must win you. I've had to clench my teeth to keep from betraying what you mean to me. If I didn't love you so madly, Oscar, you'd think more of me. That's what's so cruel. You despise the women who give their souls to be near you. There's not a trace of the Helen I was before I met you. You're taking my life with you Oscar!

Gerardo: Helen! I've explained. I have a contract.

Helen: Contract?! Contracts're made to be broken. You're using your damn contract as a weapon to murder me! I'm not afraid of your contracts. Let me go with you Oscar and we'll see about contracts. Let him sue you. He won't dare. If he does I'll kill myself.

> **Gerardo,** *who has been practising voice exercises, takes her hand.*

Gerardo: Helen, we've no right to possess each other. I don't belong to myself. I belong to my art.

Helen: Art? Don't talk to me about your art! What do I care about your art! I've only become involved in your stupid art to attract your attention. A man like you wasn't created to make a clown of himself on stage every night. It's degrading. I think you should be ashamed of it, instead of boasting all over the place. Still, I'm willing to overlook your being an artist and everything, after all I'm in love with you. I'd do the same if you were a criminal or a bankrupt.

Gerardo: Thank you.

Helen: You see how I've lost control of myself. Yes I'd still lie in the dust before you as I do now, even if you were a criminal! Still face death as I do now, even if you were a bankrupt! Yes, even then! Don't tell me I don't love you.

Gerardo: You facing death. Come Helen, women with a hunger for life like yours, don't shoot themselves. You leave that to others, the poor, lost and forgotten.

Helen: When did I say I was going to shoot myself? When did I say that? I haven't the courage. What I said was, I would die if you didn't take me with you. It's just as though one dies from a disease. Because I can live only if I'm with you! I can live without everything else—without home, without children, but not without you. *(she grabs his lapels and jerks him close and they fall on the floor)* Oscar, I can't live without you!

Gerardo: Keep calm Helen, please. They won't accept your hysteria as sufficient legal excuse for me to break my contract. Look, I've ten minutes left, but if you don't behave yourself I'm leaving now.

Helen: Oh I want the world to see me lying here! Let them all see!

Gerardo: Think of the risk.

Helen: I've nothing left to risk.

Gerardo: You'll lose your social position.

Helen: All I can lose is you. And life itself.

He tries to get up but she pushes him over.

Gerardo: What about those you love?

Helen: I love no-one but you.

Gerardo: What about your children?

She scrambles up.

Helen: Who took them away from me?! Who robbed my children of a mother?!

Gerardo: I suppose *I* made advances to *you*?

Helen: Never! I wouldn't've allowed it. I was a married woman. It wouldn't have been proper. No, I just threw myself at you just as I'm throwing myself at you now. No husband or children could stop me. If I die I shall at least have tasted life! Thank you, Oscar. Because of you I've come to know myself at last. Thank you!

Gerardo: Helen . . . now listen calmly.

Helen: Yes, yes, there're only ten minutes left.

Gerardo *(looking at watch)*: Eight and a half actually. Now listen.

He gets up.

Helen: I don't ask you to love me. Only let me breathe the same air as you!

Gerardo: Helen, you can't apply the conventional rules to a man like me. I've known society women from every country in Europe. They made scenes too when I had to leave them. But when the time came, I always knew what I had to do. I left. One has one's duty. You as well as me. And duty is the highest law.

Helen: By this time I think I know what the highest law is.

Gerardo: What is it then? Not love I hope? That's what every woman says. I'd like to live like a turtle dove too—though I'm told they're really quite vicious birds. But as long as I'm alive, I have to do my duty and earn a living.

Helen: So you won't give me back my life?

Gerardo: Of course I'll give you back your life. What good is it to me? Take it! But please, don't make more of all this than it is. How can you humiliate yourself so? Where's your pride? You'd've treated me with contempt, if I'd fallen in love with you. In the eyes of society I'm nothing. A clown! Would you fling your life away on a man whom hundreds of women have loved before you and hundreds will after you? It'll look ridiculous if you kill yourself.

Helen: I know, but what can I do?

Gerardo: Helen, Helen, I've given you all I can. Be sensible, Helen. One often thinks one's going to die. But one gets over it. Accept life's glorious fortuitousness. We didn't meet because we loved each other. We loved each other because we happened to meet. Do you really blame me for seeing you when you called with that excuse about wanting me to listen to your voice? You knew I couldn't refuse. Your beauty, elegance, grace . . . Tell me, were you certain I'd give in when you came?

Helen: How can I remember? That was a week ago.

Gerardo: Ask yourself a question, Helen: what choice is left to a man of honour in such a situation? You're known as a beautiful, desirable woman. If I'd refused to see you I'd've got myself the reputation of an unsociable lout. If I *had* seen you and then pretended I didn't understand what you wanted, I'd be taken as an idiot. And if I'd kept on refusing you there might have been whispers. I refuse one woman, perhaps I refused all women, etc, etc. I could've explained everything calmly to you, just as I'm explaining it now. But you'd've been insulted, called me vain, conceited. If I'd said 'no', however politely, I'd've made an enemy for life, a target for your sarcasm. So, I had the choice, to make an enemy who despised me or an enemy who, at least, respected me. *(he strokes her hair)* Helen, I didn't feel like being despised by such a beautiful woman. Your social position gave you the opportunity to seduce me. You took it, that's all.

Helen: Words! Words! Words! I'm choking I tell you! I'm a woman of the world—more or less. After all I've given birth to two children. What would you say if I went off and made another man as happy as I've made you? What would you say Oscar? What would you say?

Gerardo: Say? Nothing. Helen, I've five minutes.

Helen *(falling)*: Oscar! It's my life! Save me. It's the last time I'll ask you. Don't take my life. You don't know what you're doing! You're mad Oscar! You detest me because I love you. Save me! Save me!

Though she keeps flopping back onto her knees, **Gerardo** *finally manages to pull her upright.*

Gerardo: How old are your children?

Helen: Four and six.

Gerardo: Both girls?

Helen: Boys.

Gerardo: Have you no pity for them?

Helen: NO!

Gerardo: Suppose I was as unreasonable as you and thought I was in love with one particular woman and no-one else would do? I couldn't marry her or take her with me. Yet I must leave. You can see the problem?

Helen: Yes . . . Yes . . . I can see . . .

Gerardo: You say you can't live without me. But how many men do you know? The more you know the lower your opinion'll be of them. Soon it'll be as low as mine is of women. Then you wouldn't dream of killing yourself for a man.

Helen: You think I'm like *you*. But I'm not!

Gerardo: No. Everybody loves his own kind of person. They're easy enough to find.

Helen: And when one has found one's own kind and discovered he's worthless?

Gerardo: Helen, I won't have you talk about your husband like that.

Helen: My *husband*?

Gerardo: It isn't his fault. Every young girl is free to choose. There's no power on earth can make a girl belong to a man if she doesn't want to. On the deepest level, women's rights can't be flouted that way. It's the sort of nonsense women who have sold themselves for money, security or whatever, would like the world to believe, so they can escape their obligations.

Helen: And that would be a breach of contract I suppose?

Gerardo: Yes. When I sell myself I deliver what's paid for. They're at least dealing with an honest man.

Helen: So someone who's in love isn't honest.

Gerardo: No, love is for those who can't face the world, dreamers with too much imagination. Love is for second-rate poets who can't live without drooling over some half-wit with thick ankles. Love is for the incompetents, the Mark Antony's who lose an Empire and say it's well lost for love. Love is for the well-fed, go ask a beggar about love. Love is for the liars and the self-deceivers, the solitary and selfish, the weak and cowardly. Love is for those who need *excuses*. In the real world where I live, if two people come together, they know exactly why and how much it's worth in hard cash. They don't ask for love! *(he feels his throat tenderly and sings a practice note)* Me . . . Me . . . Me. Helen, once and for all. Would you sacrifice your own happiness and that of your family for this?

Helen: No.

Gerardo: Will you neglect your duties as a wife and mother?

Helen: No.

Gerardo: Are you going to keep arguing with me?

Helen: No.

Gerardo: Are you going to die because of me?

Helen: No.

Gerardo: Will you break that promise?

Helen: No.

Gerardo: Is there any reason I can't leave town now?

Helen: No.

Gerardo: Shall we kiss each other once more?

Helen: Yes—yes—yes—yes—yes—yes!

She grabs him and kisses him passionately.

Gerardo: Helen, I'll be here again next year.

Helen: Next year . . . Yes . . . Next year . . .

As he moves away to pick up the cloak he does not see her take a gun from her muff and point it at him. She changes her mind, puts the gun to her mouth and shoots herself. The mirror behind her shatters. Blood pours out of her mouth as she falls slowly to the floor. **Gerardo** *stares at her in horror.*

Gerardo: Helen. How could you? After you *promised*?

There is a knock on the door Up Stage Centre and the **Page Boy** *enters.*

Page Boy: Sir, about your luggage . . . *(he sees the body and the blood)* Dead?

Gerardo: Get the Hotel Manager.

Page Boy: Leave it to me, sir, I know exactly what to do.

He hurries out. **Gerardo** *stares at the body.*

Gerardo: No consideration for anyone but yourself, Helen. Self-indulgent to the end. You do exactly what you want and leave others to take the consequences. *(he looks mechanically at his watch)* What about me, the man you said you loved? Where does it leave me? Up to my neck. You were too romantic. Romanticism's a disease more deadly than typhus. The Germans get it worst. Always having to kill themselves or somebody else. You never had any sense of proportion, Helen.

Müller, *the Hotel Manager, hurries in with the* **Page Boy.** *He bends down and quickly examines* **Helen.**

Müller: Another one eh?

Gerardo: Send for the police! If I leave her now I'm a beast and if I stay I'm a pauper, ruined. They'll break me for breaking my contract. The police! Get the police!

Müller *rises and gestures discreetly to the* **Page Boy,** *who* *hurries out*

Müller: Calm yourself, sir. Everything's being attended to. The police and doctor are being notified.

Gerardo: Doctor? Yes . . . And the police. I must be arrested.

Müller: Quite so, sir. But she did shoot herself didn't she?

Gerardo: Of course she shot herself. You don't think I did it do you? But if I'm arrested it might count as a legal excuse for breaking my contract. At least I think it might. If it doesn't then I'm . . . *(looks at watch)* I've got one minute, ten seconds. Helen . . . Helen . . .

Müller: Calm yourself sir. We've great experience in these matters. We have at least two er, accidents, a month. More during the season. It's quite the chic thing to do. You'll see the police, just a few routine enquiries, then . . .

Gerardo: Why haven't my trunks been taken? *(he rushes to the body, kneels down beside it)* No, Helen I won't go. Helen, I'm with you, Helen. The least I can do is stay, my darling.

The **Valet** *hurries in Up Stage Centre.*

Valet: Sir, it's time you left, your carriage is at the door.

Gerardo *(jumping up)*: What about my trunks?

Valet: I'll take them, sir. Does the lady feel faint?

Gerardo: I can't stay Herr Müller. You explain to the authorities. Madame came in, shot herself and I have to sing *Tristan.*

Müller: But they'll want to question you. Certain minor formalities you understand.

Gerardo: I have to sing *Tristan.*

He stuffs money into **Müller's** *hand.*

Müller: Well, perhaps I could . . .

Gerardo *(confidentially)*: Tell me, Herr Müller, do you think this will hurt me professionally? What am I saying? I won't go! It's unthinkable! I can miss a train for her if she can shoot herself for me. Helen . . . *(he drops on his knees beside* **Helen** *and lifts her up in his arms)* Helen . . . Don't you hear me, Helen . . . The doctor'll be here any minute Helen . . . It's Oscar . . . Your Oscar.

Müller: Should I send the carriage away then, sir?

The **Page Boy** *runs back in Up Stage Centre.*

63

Page Boy: I can't find the police, sir.

Gerardo: No. I can't wait. I must sing *Tristan* tomorrow.

He dumps **Helen** *on the floor again with a thud, gets up, clicks his fingers for the* **Valet** *to follow him and exits determinedly. The lights dim down slowly as* **Müller** *and the* **Page Boy** *gather round the body on the floor and* **Gerardo** *is heard singing exquisitely, with full orchestra, an aria from 'Tristan and Isolde' in the gathering darkness.*

CURTAIN